I0539674

SOUL FOOD IN A2

FOOTBRAWL AND BEYOND

SOUL FOOD IN A2

FOOTBRAWL AND BEYOND

COACH PAUL TEST

Kravitz & Sons
INNOVATORS IN PUBLISHING, MARKETING AND ADVERTISING

Kravitz and Sons LLC
1301 Farmville Blvd, Suite 104
Greenville, NC 27834

© 2025 Coach Paul Test. All rights reserved.

No part of this book may be reproduced, stored in a retrieval system, or transmitted by any means without the written permission of the author.

Published by Kravitz and Sons LLC.

ISBN: 979-8-89639-072-5 (sc)
ISBN: 979-8-89639-071-8 (e)

Library of Congress Control Number: 2025901873

Because of the dynamic nature of the Internet, any web addresses or links contained in this book may have changed since publication and may no longer be valid. The views expressed in this work are solely those of the author and do not necessarily reflect the views of the publisher, and the publisher hereby disclaims any responsibility for them.

TABLE OF CONTENTS

INTRODUCTION

I have been coaching high school football for over forty years, and this night, October 12, 2012, is truly unforgettable. The *Ann Arbor News* refers to it as the "footbrawl," surely a nightmare for all involved. But for me, the night repeats itself many, many times.

Each time, a reminder that I am not in control of all that goes on in my life, but God is in control, and God is my vindicator. Ann Arbor Pioneer High School versus Ann Arbor Huron High School has been a great rivalry for many years and a rivalry that I've been a part of since 1980, when I joined Chuck Lori and Ann Arbor Pioneer. For me, it began when Chuck had asked my former high school football coach, Bill McCartney, for a defensive coordinator. Coach Mac was the then-defensive coordinator at the University of Michigan, under Bo Schembechler. Coach Mac recommended to Chuck to give me a call in the summer of 1980. That summer, I was doing my student teaching at Cranbrook Institute in Bloomfield Hills, Michigan, in a program called Horizons Upward Bound. I lived on campus at Cranbrook Institute with students from Detroit high schools, including Detroit Cass Tech, St. Martin DePorres, and others. Chuck Lori is a man I had the pleasure of coaching football with from 1980 until his untimely passing in 2003, when oddly enough, both Chuck and I were coaching in Ann Arbor Huron High School.

As it were, Chuck Lori would more than likely have been the new head football coach at Ann Arbor Huron in 2003. Late January, Chuck and I were speaking on the phone on a Friday night for two hours, discussing the staff and the Huron program. Chuck was excited, and so was I. The athletic director at the time was Ms. Jane Bennett. She had asked me to consider being the head football coach at Ann Arbor Huron. I thanked her but told her the man she wanted was Chuck Lori. Ms. Bennett knew Chuck's reputation and was excited. Chuck was head football coach at Pioneer when we won two class-A state championships, 1984 and 1987, beating both Dearborn Fordson and Detroit Catholic Central. At the time, I was Chuck's defensive coordinator and associate head coach; we worked quite well together, with two totally different personalities.

1984 Class A state champs, Top: Mike Holt, Keith Arnold, Paco Evangelista, Mike Butler, Vince Wortman, kneeling: Devon Wilson, Hollis Smith, David Hargrow

Chuck Lori was raised in Caldwell, Ohio, a small rural town in the southeastern corner of Ohio. Chuck played his college football at Kent State University, in Ohio, for Coach Don James, who coached at the University of Michigan under Bo and who later went on to have great success at the University of Washington. Chuck began coaching football in high school in Mansfield, Ohio. He then moved to Mishawaka Penn High School, in Mishawaka, Indiana. He was a defensive coordinator there for several years before becoming the head coach at Blackford County, Indiana, where he won a state championship in 1979. Again Chuck took over the reins at Ann Arbor Pioneer in 1980, the year I joined him. Former sportswriter for the *Ann Arbor News* John Barton wrote an article in the early 1980s, entitled "The Odd Couple." John elaborated on the differences between Chuck and me. Chuck had his beginnings in rural Southeast Ohio, out in the country, while I was much more used to living in the suburbs and city life. The first afternoon I met Chuck, in the athletic office at Pioneer, Chuck told me he lives, eats, drinks, and sleeps football. Although football had been very important to me, it didn't run my life. And although I had enjoyed college football in Pittsburgh, I also enjoyed getting away from it for a while.

In 1978, I coached the CYO football program at Divine Child School. We had an undefeated season, and defensively, we were unscored upon; we did not give up a point all season. Now this was exciting, but what I really enjoyed was the interaction with the kids, the intensity, storytelling, and laughter; it was all about the relationships. Even today, when I speak to high school football players about why playing high school football is so exciting, the most exciting part are the relationships that you build while you play.

In 2012, I had three former players coaching with me, and again oddly enough, two were from Ann Arbor Pioneer and one was from Ann Arbor Huron River Rats. All three were young African American men; one has even said, "You have been like a father to me." In 2011, one of our starting inside linebackers, Maurice, also known as Mo, called me on Father's Day a year after he graduated to tell me, "You've been like a father to me." He, too, was a young African American. For some reason, I believe God gave me an ability to really connect in a positive way with the black athletes that I've coached. It brings joy to my heart when after having spoken to these young black coaches on my staff, we end the conversation with God bless you. This means the world to me, because it demonstrates not just respect for a relationship but an appreciation of our heavenly Father. Having coached in Ann Arbor most of my life, there is much diversity in race, color, and creed, and I love that. To see a healthy appreciation for the differences, with a healthy respect for those differences, be it black, white, Asian, Christian, Muslim, Jew, or a secular viewpoint. There are many social issues that we face today that cause anger bitterness, frustration, and/or detachment by people. This is sad because all of us have faults and need God's grace and mercy, his unmerited favor.

When I pray the Lord's prayer, I am reminded, "Forgive me my sins as I have forgiven those who have sinned against me." I am only at peace when I have forgiveness, and I have a forgiving heart toward others. In the footbrawl incident, I have forgiven all involved, especially the head coach at Huron. Recently the Ann Arbor Huron athletic director stopped by the M Den at Briarwood Mall. We spoke kindly, and at one point, I discussed coaching with the former Ann Arbor Huron coach.

She responded, "He would never coach with you." Once again, I have no control over what someone else does, but that does not mean that I'm not going to do the right thing regardless of what someone else does. As a matter of fact, he and I spoke in 2010 about me being his defensive coordinator at Ann Arbor Huron High School. Although I was interested, I chose, at the time, not to pursue it further. So I always felt that there was a healthy respect between us, when possibly he was annoyed at the results of our 2011 and 2012 seasons. As I've stated, I've never gotten mad at the other coach when being on the losing end of a contest; rather I've gotten mad at myself when we lose because I have not done a good job in preparing my team. Preparation and attention to detail is the key to winning football games and to being a successful man or woman in life. So with that said, I still wish him all the best and God's blessings, not only for his sake but for my peace of mind as well.

The three years while I was Ann Arbor Huron—2000, 2001, and 2002—as defensive coordinator, we beat Ann Arbor Pioneer during the regular season in lopsided victories.

As the head freshman football coach at Ann Arbor Huron in 1998 and 1999, we defeated Ann Arbor Pioneer freshman in lopsided victories. The year 1998 was the first undefeated season Ann Arbor Huron football ever had. In 2000, Coach Paul Verska asked me to coordinate the defense for him. Coach Verska have done a great job at Ann Arbor Huron High School. As a matter of fact, in 1992, we faced each other as head coaches—my first round as head coach at Ann Arbor Pioneer High School—and we were on the losing end of a 46–16 defeat. One of my worst defeats ever. Paul had done a great job of lulling me to sleep, having met with him for a film exchange on a Sunday evening. Coach Verska said, "Maybe I should be coaching over here with you at Pioneer."

I thought, *He thinks* we're pretty good, and that was a big mistake because we got our butt kicked; we were unprepared. Up until that point, we had had a better season than they had, but if you take anybody lightly, that's a big mistake.

In 2001, Chuck Lori joined the staff at Huron as the offensive coordinator, and Ann Arbor Huron, under Head Coach Verska, had two playoff seasons. In 2001, we led the area on offense and defense. Offensively we had more points per game and yardage than any other team, and defensively we had given up fewer points and less yardage than any other team. I will speak of it in a later chapter, but we had cousins Jeff Jenkins, a running back who attended Notre Dame University on a scholarship, and Carl Tabb, a wide receiver who attended the University of Michigan. Both were phenomenal athletes and very good students. I believe Carl is currently a pediatrician locally, and Jeff is doing quite well for himself as well.

The competitive environment that existed between Pioneer and Huron, I had always viewed as a wholesome situation. A great example was 1987, when Ann Arbor Huron upset Pioneer in the last game of the season when they blocked a field goal, and Chucky Phillips ran it back for a touchdown. We at Pioneer had been leading the entire game. Late in the second half, Coach Lori had received a few fifteen-yard penalties for losing his cool, and a poor punt allowed the River Rats great field position for a touchdown.

5

But the crowd went nuts when Phillips ran into the end zone as time ran out. I was devastated by the loss, but our kids were resilient and were getting ready for the playoffs the following week. Back then, Pioneer versus Huron was always the last game of the season; now it is not. I believe that lessens some of the tense competitiveness of the game.

The good news for us, in 1987, was we went on to win the state championship against Detroit Catholic Central, three to nothing. That was an exciting season for me as the defensive coordinator because we shut out CC twice in week 3 and in the state championship final.

In 2012, during a 35–6 victory, the River Rat head coach became incensed when a freshman quarterback threw a long pass late in the game. The pass was incomplete but ruled as interference, and we had a first down on the River Rat end of the field. After this long pass, the Huron coach began to yell across the field, quite agitated. One of his players had already been evicted from the game for calling a Pioneer player the N-word.

It was a physical game all night, and there were a number of personal foul penalties. In 2011, following a 50–7 Pioneer victory, the Huron coach walked away and didn't shake my hand. In retrospect, I may have done that in 2012, but I didn't.

Instead, I apologized for the pass and said, "I did not call the play."

He responded by cussing me out, "What do you mean you didn't call the f——play, who is in charge of your f——team?"

One of my assistant coaches, upon hearing him speak to me that way, ran over and pushed him away from me, then bedlam ensued for the next fifteen to twenty minutes; and although it was ugly, no one was seriously hurt. I was sad to see one young man got cut during the altercation. This assistant coach said if it happened again, he would've done the same thing because the River Rat coach was being disrespectful, and another assistant said if he wouldn't have done it, I would've. There were no punches or kicks thrown by the coaches, just pushing. The officials at the game and parents in the stands heard and saw most of what went on. I wish we could do it over, but life doesn't work that way, and now it is history.

That same season in the Super Bowl, when the two Harbaugh brothers were coaching their respective teams, the 49ers and the Ravens, a brawl broke out for several minutes. The intensity was very high, and emotions were also peaking. After a while, the players were pulled apart, and the game continued. In our incident, some of which was filmed, a Huron player actually is shown hitting one of our players before my assistant ever pushed the Huron coach. This was sort of swept under the rug and blame assigned elsewhere.

One of my offensive assistants had called the long pass play while I was watching (I had removed my headphones and usually spoke primarily to the defensive coaches). I had not called the play; the play was a pass play deep, but the pass was incomplete, and after the Huron coach was screaming across the field, I ran down the sideline to our offense and yelled out to them to take a knee. We proceeded to take a knee until time ran out. This is the most salient point that seems to have gone unnoticed, because we could've tried to score again but did not. Also when substitutes enter the game, they want to play and compete just like a starter because they work on it all week long at practice. You cannot tell them to go in and give your mediocre effort. I've been on the losing end a few times in lopsided losses and never blamed the other coach but rather blamed myself for not preparing my team better.

I believe it was 1984, Pioneer was playing Monroe at Pioneer, and up by a large margin, when our third-string quarterback threw a long pass and completed it. The Monroe coach walked halfway across the field with his hands in the air, yelling, "Why, Chuck, why!"

Chuck responded, "If you coach your kids up, you won't get your butt kicked."

I know times have changed, but I believe there's nothing wrong with tough competition that is encompassed in sportsmanship. I asked my assistant after the game, "Why did you throw the long pass?"

And he responded, "You said you wanted to kick their butt." I responded that was before the game, trying to get our players ready to play mentally and psychologically.

Prior to the game, I brought our players together and said, "You guys are not ready to play, and you'll get your butts kicked and make their season in doing so." Our kids responded well with the victory despite having lost half a dozen starters that year to injury.

There was a time between Coaches Bo Schembechler and Woody Hayes, following the game between Ohio State and Michigan, when a sportscaster asked why Coach Hayes (after Ohio State scored a touchdown) had gone for two, late in the game, up by a lot.

Woody responded, "Because I could not go for three."

Maybe this was a little over the top, but I always cherished a rivalry Bo coached for Woody and was an Ohio native, from Barberton, Ohio, but it did not prevent him from always wanting to beat the Buckeyes.

I wish all of the student athletes from Pioneer and Huron only the best and wish it had not happened. Back in 2012, I got on the PA system at Pioneer and read an apology to the students and staff. I took responsibility for the incident and apologized. To this day, the Ann Arbor newspaper still reports that I resigned as a result of the brawl at Huron's field. This is not true. I did not resign nor was I forced to resign as a result of that incident. Ms. Eve Clare can testify to this, the current AD at AA Pioneer. This is poor reporting on their part, but who wants to be bored with the truth! All involved, including the game officials, know that I did nothing to initiate a fight or an argument.

I also attended a meeting at Ann Arbor Huron High School, led by the Huron AD, and she and the Pioneer AD met with both coaches and captains from both teams. The intention of the meeting was to heal some wounds; the problem was there was no apology spoken about or offering of forgiveness about what happened. No accountability was mentioned regarding what really happened that night. So it was kind of counterproductive to meet when there was no opportunity to speak the truth about what happened. The only profitable conversation involved some community service to heal the communities' view of the incident. Lots of people commented on the incident on the Internet blogs. Most of them had really no idea of what really happened that night. Many of them didn't even appear to be football enthusiasts, rather pointers of fingers, blame, and guilt. I just hope that the people that were doing this receive more mercy when their time comes on this earth or when they leave this earth and the wrongs they've done.

One blogger was a parent of one of our players who had decided to quit late in the season. He was angry at his son's playing time and how his season had gone. I understood his frustration, but quitting was not the answer to the problem and rarely ever is. I would have done some things differently with his son but hindsight is always 20-20. The son was more responsible than the father was. It amazes me how much can be said online when there is little to no knowledge of what really transpired and no accountability for what is said.

The one main thing that I took from the entire incident is I am not in control of what goes on in my life every moment. We want to be in control, especially as coaches. But the truth is we are not in control of what goes on around us day to day. It requires a good deal of humility to acknowledge this and hope and trust that a good God is ultimately in control. This is not to say that we are not responsible for our actions, because we are; but many times, circumstances happen beyond our control, and without faith and hope in God, it is easy to become disillusioned or disheartened by events.

This is why many people who commented on the game online wanted to find blame and point fingers at all involved. I believe many don't accept my premise that God is in control. Consequently the only alternative is to want to assign fault, blame, and guilt. It truly was a humbling experience in many ways, especially since I had prided myself in demonstrating integrity and honesty as a coach. Being far from perfect and recognizing now that the whole experience has only made me more determined to surrender my will to God, who is in control. I am lucky that I am not in control of all that happens around me. So indeed, "all things work together for good to those who believe." One of the most frustrating elements to the ordeal was the young men who were initially charged with crimes. Thank God they were not charged; ultimately they were exonerated. It truly breaks my heart that they went through the turmoil of court proceedings. But by the grace of God, all charges were dropped. I spent many mornings in the courthouse praying for them and trying to show my support.

There definitely was pain and gain. The pain was obvious, the embarrassment, the injuries, the memory it left for the fans, and especially for children in the stands. But the gain is not quite so obvious—recognizing my need to turn control over every day to my good God. If I had a dime for every person who has said to me, "I know you didn't start that debacle, I know your character," I would be a rich man.

Much went in to my development as a coach over the years. My mentors, along with Chuck Lori, were Bill McCartney, Gary Moeller Milan Vooletich, Lloyd Carr, and others. While I learned a lot of football from all of them, only McCartney developed my spiritual growth. Although I could walk literally across the street to Michigan to learn football, Coach Mac would recite Bible verses and pray with me about my relationship with Jesus Christ. Nothing was and is more important than that relationship. Faith is the substance of things hoped for the evidence of that which is not seen! St. Paul tells us here in Hebrews that what I hope for will come to pass if I am living for the Lord. That doesn't mean that I'm going to get everything I want, but I will get what I need; and thank God he knows what I need better than I do.

There is a battle going on every day—spiritual warfare. The enemy wants to destroy us, and God came to save us from that enemy and our own selfish desires. This is a truth that I know, in my heart, will follow me until my pilgrimage is over; but thank God that greater is He that is in me than he that is in the world.

Beginnings

Grandpa Paolo Testa & Grandma Giovanella Testa

Paolo Testa and Giovanella (Carano) Testa settled in Youngstown, Ohio, at the turn of the century, the 1900s. They traveled from Italy, the small mountain town of Carovilli, near the bigger town of Campobosso, about the size of Ann Arbor. My grandfather Paolo, whom I am named after, worked for over fifty years in the steel mill in Youngstown, while my grandmother Genny ran a boarding house and rented a shoe store, a grocery store, and a used car lot. They were Abruzzi, or Abruzzese, at the time; although now Carovilli, named after a Roman soldier, is part of the province of Molise/Molisano since the 1950s.

Paul (2 yrs.) Dad/ Sam Test

My father, Samuel, real name Salvatore Pasquale Testa, took my two older brothers, Sam and Dennis, and me to the steel mills to instill in us the importance of an education so we wouldn't end up working in a steel mill. He made his point, and all three of us graduated from college and procured good jobs. I hope that our country can return to that hard-work ethic where all people can achieve their dreams if they work for them. My father had two brothers. Pasquale Salvatore Testa, also known as Dr. P. S. Test (Patrick), was a head surgeon at Mansfield General Hospital. He graduated Phi Beta Kappa, from the Ohio State

University, as a physician. He was a captain in the army during World War II. My father's other brother was Dominic Testa, a wonderful man with a great sense of humor, who lived in Youngstown, Ohio, all his life, moving from 308 Byron Street, in Youngstown, to the suburb of Boardman, Ohio.

While my Uncle Pat had no children, Uncle Nick and his wife, Aunt Angeline, had two children: Jeanne and Dominic, or Nicky. Due to some congenital issue early in life, my uncle Nick and his wife could not speak or hear. But that did not keep them from communicating with us in wonderful ways. It also taught myself and my siblings to learn sign language, while my Aunt Angeline could read lips very well. My uncle Nick could've been an actor because he would often act out scenes of what he wanted to convey to us. Oddly enough, this is the profession my cousin, his son, Nicky, chose to pursue, acting and entertainment. Nicky was a musician most of his life and undertook acting later in life. I was very grateful for having great relatives and their heritage of Italian culture from my father.

You can see why I grew up an Ohio State fan, having had relatives in Ohio and a father and uncle that attended OSU. As I will talk about it in later chapters, it's odd that in 1979, I moved to Ann Arbor, Michigan, home of the Michigan Wolverines. Here I would spend the next thirty-six years or more, pulling for the Michigan Wolverine to win championships, which they did in 1997 under head coach Lloyd Carr. Coach Carr's children attended Ann Arbor St. Francis School, and I had the pleasure of working with all three of his children, as well as getting to know his wife, who often worked in the school office. My former high school coach, Bill McCartney, was instrumental in bringing Coach Carr to Michigan as the secondary coach.

In the 1980s, I learned a lot about defensive back play and techniques from Coach Carr. Again I was truly blessed to learn from that caliber of coach and have those connections.

Diverting from beginnings momentarily, I will always love the quote from Dr. Martin Luther King Jr. in his famous speech, when he said, "I dream of the day when my people are not judged by the color of our skin but by the content of her character." The irony of the entire recent Michael Brown incident, where he was sadly shot and killed, is indicative of not adhering to the latter part of that quote. He, Michael Brown, had been in a store shoplifting and roughhousing a small Asian man. Now this does not mean that he should've been killed, but he certainly was not displaying the good character the Dr. King spoke about. He had put himself in a precarious situation by his own doing. Because we are not in control of all that goes on around us is important that we use wisdom. Soul sense or wisdom is an ability to look deeper at a situation than just on the surface level and seek to find the essence of understanding that is often hidden under all the minutia of everyday life.

FAMIGLIA

My parents, Sam and Denise Test, moved from Canton, Ohio, to Dearborn, Michigan.

It took ten years for my parents to have their first child, Sam Jr., to which my mother gave great thanks to God. She followed Sam with Dennis, Paul, and Janine, my sister.

Paul, Denny, Sam/Bub (kids)

We were all within about five years of each other. My mother, who is, in my mind, still the sweetest woman that ever lived, was so grateful she went to church after each birth.

Now I would like to make the first mention of our title, *Soul Food*. My mother was born and raised in San Antonio, Texas. She was a wonderful cook, and as children, we ate corn bread, collard greens, with ham hocks and okra gumbo. After meeting my father, she also was taught to make wonderful Italian food by my grandmother. Whenever we travel to Youngstown, Ohio, we were served courses of food by my grandmother, who would repeat the term *mangia, mangia* (eat, eat).

I was a young child at the time when we moved to Michigan but grew up as a devoted fan of Ohio State, Cleveland Browns, and the Cleveland Indians. My father worked his way through the Ohio State University to earn his degree. We would watch the Buckeyes play on TV, and Dad would hold his buckeye. We had a saying at the bar my father built in the basement; it said, "Even on the grass, we'll beat their ass." At night, I would listen to the Cleveland Indians on the radio. They were always good enough to keep me interested but always failed down the stretch.

Once in Dearborn, we attended Divine Child School, two blocks down the street on North Silvery Lane. Now Divine Child School was quite new, and as a child, every Sunday afternoon, we went to Dearborn Edsel Ford High School to watch the Falcons of Divine Child compete in football. They were quite good, coached by Tony Versacci, a young and enthusiastic, as well as innovative, coach. His first several seasons, Divine Child was undefeated and exciting to watch. With the likes of running back Nick Ross, quarterback Phil Baster, Mike Kalis, Gary Danielson, who later played at the University of Purdue and the NFL and is currently a TV sports broadcaster, running back Ed Puishes, and many, many more. In 1970, the captain and standout player would be my brother Dennis Test. As they demolished one school after another, they moved up into the higher class of football; at the time, it was called AA. The most exciting game I saw as a young child was when Divine Child upset a very talented Detroit St. Ambrose team, coached by former

Michigan State University and Pittsburgh Steeler coach George Perles. Coach Tony Versacci had revved up the excitement at a pep assembly so high that I believe every student in the school could've taken the kickoff back for a touchdown, which is what exactly happened on the opening kickoff. Coach Versacci was a wonderful motivator and way ahead of his time. He also hired the future successor to him, Bill McCartney.

As the youngest of three boys, I looked up to Sam and Dennis. I first watched Sam play offensive line on the Dearborn Lions and later watched Dennis on the Dearborn Lions as well. I followed and played on the Dearborn Lions at the pony, JV, and varsity levels. I always preferred defense and loved to tackle. My father always taught me to wrap up their legs and hit them low, since I was small; I followed his advice and had success tackling. At school, we would play tackle pom-pom at lunch hour. You would run across the grass field and see who was left standing at the end. Today that would be illegal—too rough, too dangerous—someone might get hurt; sometimes we did. But this was how we got tough. I played four years with the Dearborn Lions before joining the Divine Child CYO in eighth grade.

As I got into high school, my brother Sam was graduating, and although he played football, he excelled in golf and was an All-City golfer at DC. He attended Michigan State University in East Lansing and studied business. My next oldest brother, Dennis, and I were in high school about the same time, and he excelled in football. We did play basketball together when he was in eighth grade. I was the first sixth grader to make the eighth-grade basketball team, so we did participate together. But in high school, he was the *man*, both at school and in the neighborhood. Nobody wanted to mess with him on the streets because they knew they'd get their butts kicked. He was tough; his nickname was Julio by some, because he had the dark-Italian look, with olive skin, dark hair and combed it up high in the front, like Ricky Nelson or Elvis, only curlier. While sitting at a basketball game with my father, someone on Bishop Gallagher kept pushing him under the boards consistently. I could tell it was annoying Denny, so Dennis decided he had had enough and punched him in the face and knocked him out; his tooth went through his cheek, and there was quite a bit of blood. My father ran out into the court, ready to throw down himself. Dad was a gentleman, but the Youngstown came out at the right time. Denny's junior year, my grandfather passed away, and my grandmother came to live with us. Coach Versacci came by the house to offer his condolences to my parents and to Dennis. It meant a lot to my family that Coach Versacci came by. Dennis ended up playing that Sunday in the football game at Edsel Ford High School. Coach Versacci was smart; he knew that Dennis would want to play, especially after he came by to show that he cared. He was a class act. My grandmother only lived a few weeks before she passed away. After having spent over seventy years together, her heart was truly broken.

Traveling to the funeral of my grandfather Paolo, my grandmother chanted, *"Paolo Mio, Paolo Mio,"* (My Paul, my Paul), singing it all the way there and all the way home. She told my mother she did not want to live anymore because she had lost her dearly beloved Paolo. Dennis and I hung out a lot and went to the school dances together. Word was the dances didn't start till the Test brothers arrived. We would get a circle going at the dance and take turns dancing inside the circle, generally to soul music. Soul music for R & B, for rhythm and blues, is what I enjoy the most, and so did Denny. Soul food, soul music, and feeding the soul all make life interesting, rich and enjoyable as we go through life. The dance I remember the most featured a group from Inkster called Cornell Turner and the Soul Syndicate. They were fantastic; they would play Sly and the Family Stone, Sam and Dave, James Brown, and many other soulful groups. We had some interesting dances, including the bump, the turtle that my brother Dennis created, mashed potatoes popcorn, Detroit shuffle, chicken walk, cold duck, and many other improvisational moves.

Mom Test, Paul, Dennis Test

His senior year, Dennis was captain of the Divine Child football team, along with Steve Burton, and went on to be captain of the Detroit News All-State Dream Team. He was recruited all over the country by prominent colleges, such as Michigan, Michigan State, Purdue, Stanford, and the University of Southern California. He chose USC, and now as the old group Kool & The Gang would sing, he was "Hollywood Swinging." John McKay was the head coach at USC, and the assistant coach that recruited Dennis was Wayne Fonts, former head coach of the Detroit Lions. While being recruited by the University of Michigan, Assistant Coach George Manns was responsible for communicating with Dennis.

One evening, Bo Schembechler came to the house to speak with my father and Dennis. He came into the basement, and my dad began to talk to Bo about some of his Youngstown exploits. After my father was done, Bo turned to my brother and asked, "Well, Dennis, do you want to be a Wolverine?"

As a sophomore in high school, I was sitting downstairs, listening. After all, Bo was in our basement; it was exciting. My brother responded, "I don't know."

Bo was a very busy man and a great coach. He left without receiving a commitment from my brother. As time passed, Dennis chose USC and headed out to LA. I looked up to him a lot, so when he graduated and went to college that far away, I missed him a lot. I did go out to visit Denny my senior year in high school during spring break; I flew to LAX. For Dennis, they were involved in spring ball, and he was very busy, but I enjoyed the visit. I could certainly see how Los Angeles could entice an eighteen-year-old to head West. As Horace Greeley said, "Go west, young man." I had the excitement and pleasure to meet, at USC, Pat Haden, their QB, and Lynn Swann WR, who eventually played for the Pittsburgh Steelers and is in the NFL Hall of fame.

Paul "Soul Man"

Class B state champs, Paul (junior #11)

Meanwhile back at Divine Child, I was doing okay for myself. I had a real good junior season in football and was All-City as a defensive back safety. The *Dearborn Press and Guide* newspaper described me as a Larry Wilson-type safety; Wilson played for the St. Louis Cardinals. My junior year, I also played a little bit of running back, having a few good runs. One in particular, against Royal Oak Shrine, help put us in scoring position, a game that we won, defeating the defending AA League champs and avenging the previous season's loss. The year before my brother's senior year, Divine Child was undefeated entering into the Shrine Game, and lost. Royal Oak Shrine ran a T-formation offense featuring fullback Tim O'Bradovich, a hard-running physical fullback.

My junior year, I was assigned as a strong safety to play in the middle of the defense, at about five yards deep, just inside the two inside linebackers, and key the fullback, taking him wherever he goes from tight end to tight end. Coach Morrissey taught me well that week, and we were able to shut down O'Bradovich and win the game. My first game against U of D Jesuit High School, I had about twenty tackles, broke up a few passes, and returned kickoffs. I had a good game, and when I arrived home, my dad met me in the basement and said, "Son, would you like a beer?"

To which I replied, "Sure, Dad." It was as though I had entered into manhood, a rite of passage, where I showed my father what I was taught, and I pleased him. We were Class B state champs that year, before there were any playoff system. The *Detroit News* had us number 1 at the end of the season.

We defeated Centerline St. Clement in the Catholic League championship in a game that was never close, 28–0. I began to receive a lot of letters from colleges and received a phone call from a recruiter locally that helped out the Ohio State University. Growing up a Buckeye fan, I was very excited about this, but my senior year, they lost interest. My senior year, again I was selected to the All-City team and to the All-League team as a defensive safety. We defeated Detroit Catholic Central and won the Catholic League championship, 31–0.

Gary Forstyk, our quarterback, and Ed Kasparek both had big games offensively, throwing the ball deep, while our defense shut out the physical offense of CC. I began to get letters from colleges, and after taking a trip to Pittsburgh, Pennsylvania, for the weekend, I decided to sign the letter of intent with the Pittsburgh Panthers. I was very excited that I would be playing Division I football and only be sixty miles away from Youngstown, Ohio, where I had relatives that I could visit. This became very important to me because in January of my freshman year at Pitt, my father passed away from cancer. I had a very difficult time with that, as one could imagine, as an eighteen- year-old young man. One of the most difficult moments I've ever had was walking away from the Detroit (Tuxedo) hospital knowing that I would never see my father again, alive.

My father was kind of old school in his parenting. He could get pretty angry at times with his discipline of the children in our family. He and I especially could get pretty irritated with each other. Prior to his death, my mother told me he said, "I hope that boy knows how much I love him, despite being tough on him." I knew how much he loved me and how much I loved him, as did my brothers and sister. My mother did such a good job of caring for him while he was sick for over a year and a half. Sometimes we forget how difficult it is for the caregiver of the person who is ill, both physically and psychologically.

Because they realize they're about to be alone, although my mother knew she had the four of us as children to help her through. My father's death caused me to cop an attitude that took me a while to get over. With Dad gone, I acted like I didn't care what happened most of the time. I missed him a lot. He was a great dad and a great provider for his family.

BELLA DONNA

One of the primary motivators for me getting excited about school were the girls. While I had had the same girlfriend from eighth grade to twelfth grade, I enjoyed interacting with most of the girls at school. My girlfriend was Italian; her mother was from Italy, in the heel of the boot of Italy. She was a very bright young lady and was homecoming queen our senior year, in the fall of 1972. We had gone together for four years in high school. We broke up and never really did get back together again; although we did see each other a few times in college, it just wasn't the same. It wasn't there anymore. By the way, my sister, Janine (Dee Dee) Test, was homecoming queen in the fall of 1973, the following year. She was and is the sweetest person I know, and obviously others felt the same way about her, just like our mother.

Breaking up with my girlfriend did mess me up for a while. While I was saddened, my father did not like to see me despondent. The first time I ever saw my father cry was as we stood above his father's grave site in Youngstown, Ohio. I did not want him to be sad, so I did my best to break off from that relationship; it was good that I did. My father was a wonderful businessman. He was the manager of the Social Security office in Detroit, Michigan; he was on TV commercials and ran a big office in Detroit, where he had to hire and fire employees, a stressful job. As I previously said, Dad was a great provider and a wonderful husband and father.

The real anchor of our home was my mother, Texas star. Her mother had passed away when she was only twelve, and her father when she was eighteen. She did have three brothers that helped her get through the tough years after her parents died. While working for the government, she met my father in Baltimore, Maryland. Both Mom and Dad loved to dance; both also had a good sense of humor. They were perfect for each other. Mother could get along with anyone and certainly did with my father.

Mom and Dad taught us to have *faith*. The last word my mother spoke before she passed at age ninety-six was *faith*, and she spelled it out loud. Because her parents had died so young, my mother, after having met my dad, was indoctrinated into the Test family, so became Italian in her culture. When we were kids, my mother told the story of her and my father traveling in the deep South while my father was in the military. They were pulling an airstream trailer behind their car when the car stalled, and they were stuck on the side of a very steep hill. My mother began to pray for help during this seemingly difficult time. They were out in the middle of nowhere and unfamiliar with their surroundings. Some would say as fate would have, my mother would say as faith would have it, the first vehicle to come over the hill was indeed a tow truck, and the seemingly problematic time became nothing more than an opportunity to trust God through faith.

This story has stuck with me all of my life, and so this debacle known as the footbrawl by the *Ann Arbor* News is truly nothing more than an opportunity to share the good news about my good God. My mother had tremendous faith that she demonstrated every day of her life. She would often call upon the intercession of our dear lady, the blessed Mother of Jesus. Some Christians might say, why invoke Mary? My mother would say that her Mother Mary was a great example of what God expects of us. When Mary was confronted by the angel Gabriel during the announcement that she would be with child, Mary's response was, "Be it done unto me according to the will." Not "*my*" will, not what I want, but what do you want from me, Lord?

A good Christian brother of mine, that I taught with at Pattengill Elementary School in Ann Arbor, James Taylor, would say, "The theme song in hell will be 'I did it *my way*'!" James, an African American from Detroit, who grew up without a father but was a strong believer in Christ throughout his life. Many of his friends and associates, growing up, got into trouble with drugs and the law; he did not. One day our first year working together, he was talking to me about college and going to grad school to obtain a master's degree. I encouraged him and said, "Sure, that's a great idea. I did it myself, surely you can do it." He, in fact, did get his master's degree, and later, he said to me that nobody in his family had encouraged him to go after his master's because nobody in his family had done so. Just recently, I went to honor his mother when she passed away. It was great to see James and his family. Many former teachers were there as well, especially from Pattengill Elementary. There were also former bus drivers and school personnel that I had not seen in many years. I guess we did not care about what role we played in the school system; we all were there for the kids. We also didn't care what color someone is because at the funeral, there was a divergent group of people from all races sharing in the Christian faith ceremony.

Funny, but death can remind us that we all have the same ending regardless of what our status is here on earth. Yes, black lives matter, and yes all other lives matter as well, including that of the unborn and those who are old and with infirmities. We became great friends over the years, including involvement in a group called the Promise Keepers. The Promise Keepers was the name of a men's group that oddly enough, my former high school coach, Bill McCartney, began while he was head football coach at the University of Colorado, in Boulder, Colorado.

Promise Keepers began as a prayerful consideration in Bill McCartney's mind.

Coach Mac's intention was to cross racial barriers, denominational barriers, and to teach man to be good husbands and good fathers. The media, despite these good intentions, tried their hardest to attack Promise Keepers, but it was really quite difficult to find fault with the group, since its foundational intention was for men to treat women and children with more love and respect, not a bad idea!

The Promise Keepers group that I belonged to and interacted with for years consisted of an interesting array of characters. There was Ray Scott, former NBA player and coach at 6'10", African American; James Taylor, African American; Doc Andrews, four feet tall, a small person that was marvelous on the Dick Purtan show on the radio; former teammate at Divine Child Paul Nanasi, who played his college football at the University of Minnesota, white and big; James Edwards, an African American; and a wonderful man by the name of Leroy Madison, who lived in Hamtramck, Michigan, with his family, his son, Antonio, that I prayed for regularly at the bequest of Leroy; and myself, Paul Test.

We met twice a month for several years, generally at the office of Ray Scott in Livonia, Michigan, just off Schoolcraft Road. At one of the first meetings, Leroy began to talk and said that as a young person, he hated white people. So I looked at Leroy and asked him why. It took Leroy several minutes to answer, but with tears in his eyes, looking at me, he said, "Because I hated myself and did not have a father figure to look up to." Leroy said to me, "Nobody has ever asked me why. Thanks for asking." I believe part of the problem in this country is that most people, black and white, are afraid to talk about racial issues from the heart. So most problems, concerns, and fears continue to go on without solutions. We are afraid to ask tough questions of one another, and sometimes we are afraid of the answers we receive. We aren't going to agree on everything—no one does—but open dialogue can help to allow conversation, to listen to one another and try to have compassion for what the other person is feeling. Compassion means "to suffer with," or as some say today, "I feel ya." There is a story that I would tell my teams at both Pioneer and Huron, entitled, "The Rainbow People." It is from a book called *Storytelling*, and it has a wonderful message.

In a beautiful meadow at the bottom of a great Mountain lived a people called the Greens. They wore green clothes, lived in green homes, drove green cars and believed that God was green.

At the top of the big mountain or another people, the Blues. They wore blue clothes, Lived in blue homes, Drove blue cars and believed god was blue. Greens and blues didn't speak to each other, in fact they hated each other. Green parents would teach their grandchildren to say, Green is happy Blue is sad Greens are good blues are bad, Well the blue parents would teach their blue children to say, Blue is happy Green is said blues are good greens are bad.

Blues and greens grew up seeing each other as bad and sad, but they really didn't know each other. Some blues Went a whole lifetime without even talking to A green. They did not know each other because they stayed in their own territories they did not go to the same churches for school or shopping centers.

It's so happen one day at a green boy was walking with his father when he saw Blue boy flying his kite in their meadow. When the Blue boy saw them he became frightened and ran back toward his Mountain. But in doing so he sprained his ankle and could not walk very well. The green boy wanted to help him, what his father said, No, don't you remember what your mother and I taught you? Green is happy, Blue is sad, greens are good, blues are bad. The green boy still asks his dad if you could help the blue boy; dad how do we know the blue is bad? All I know is that he has a sprained ankle and he needs someone to help in walk home. When the green boy said this, his father turned to him saying: "Blue is the color of evil. God only loves Green. Our religion teaches us to help our own kind. Do as you're told!" A few weeks later the green boy was playing with his pet rabbit. He chased it through the tall grass and into the open fields. He played for so long that without realizing it he had crossed into Blue Land. He was about to catch the rabbit when the rascal jumped down a small cliff. The green boy went after him and is doing so caught his right leg between two big rocks. He pushed and pulled but could not move. He called for help, hoping a Green would hear him. He worried that sooner or later a blue would come by.

This thought frightened him because he had never met a blue.

As the sunlight faded, someone approached the trapped green boy. It was a blue. It was the same boy who had sprained his ankle, the who had been flying his kite in Green land. The Green boy closed his eyes waiting to be hurt by his enemy. The blue boy stood there by the Green boy for a few moments. Then he went to a tree and broke off a branch. The green boy said, "Please don't hit me with that branch", thinking that is what the Blue boy was about to do. Blue answered him, "I'm not going to it hit you." The branch is to pry loose the rocks that are holding your leg. Blue pried loose the rocks, then tore his blue shirt into long strips and tied the branch to Greens leg for support Then he helped Green boy walk home. When Green's father saw his sons leg tied with blue cloth he cursed his boy. "I do not care if you were injured," he screamed. "You should not have let a blue touch you". Although Blue knew his father was upset with him, he could not forget the blue who had helped him When his leg healed, he went into blue land to find his helper.

For a whole day Green walked in the neighborhoods of blue land. It took a lot of courage for him to do this because everywhere he went people slam doors in his face and call him names. Some young children even threw rocks at him. Finally, he found the boy who had helped him. He did not slam the door on green. He welcomed him into his home. Green was happy to see blue come but he was surprised to see that his helper had clothes that had combined the colors blue and green. "I thought that you learned Green was bad. Why are you wearing green with your blue?" asked green. "Do you remember when I helped you when you were hurt? I tore up my blue shirt to make a splint for your leg. I figured that you became part of me, and I became part of you. In helping you and talking with you, I came to see that green is as good as blue". "Won't the other blues throw rocks at you when they find out you're a green lover?" asked Green. "I don't care what people think," said blue. "It is right to help people whether they are blue or green".

The two boys became close friends. They often visited each other. They made up a new song which they taught to their children. It went like this: "Green is good but so is Blue, Purple, Yellow and Red too—All the children should be glad For there is no color that is bad"!

Little by little, more blues and greens started visiting one another. Then they began going to each other's Schools and even Churches. They even went beyond their own lands and visited the Yellows, Reds and Purples. After a while, most people didn't call themselves Greens or Blues—but simply—people. To this day, their children sing, there is no color that is bad!

Soul Food speaks to the soul and teaches us to have compassion toward all people.

Compassion literally means to suffer with. Suffering doesn't sound like a lot of fun, but sometimes the only way we can understand what someone else is going through is if we experience it ourselves. I've always loved, as a coach, telling stories that have meaning and principles. We remember stories so much better than a lecture or talk. We also have a Savior that chose to suffer and die for us. Now I am sure God could have chosen a different way of creating atonement for our sins, but he chose to suffer so that He understood exactly what we deal with in our lifetimes here on earth. The humility it took to be ridiculed and berated by those who killed him. Promise Keepers was established to help people understand one another better, racially, denominationally, familial, and marital, but most importantly, how God loves us and gave himself for us, sacrificing his only begotten Son out of love for us. What greater love is there than to lay down one's life for another ?

I pray for the Huron coach to have peace and forgiveness.

Forgiveness may be one of the most important virtues we can practice here on earth. Without forgiveness, we often harbor resentment and a vengeful attitude toward the person we feel has wronged us. This is not only bad for the person we are angry at, but it is also unhealthy for us physically, mentally, and especially spiritually. In high school football, the competitive spirit should arise from the camaraderie and relationships within your team, more so than from a dislike of your opponent. Some rivalries create more intensity, especially intercity rivalries, rivalries that have been established since childhood competition in the middle schools and in the grade schools.

It is like competing against your brother; you don't want to lose because they are family, and there is more emotion involved. Being the youngest of three boys in my family, I always had to try my hardest to even stand a chance of competing against my two older brothers. Now this doesn't mean that anger or frustration was the result or dislike for my brothers or for my opponents; rather it was because I cared about them greatly that I wanted to win, that I wanted to impress them, that I could earn their respect. This is how I envisioned the stiffest competition that we would face as a team that I was coaching, and if we lost, I wasn't angry at the opponent; I was angry at myself as a coach, that I didn't prepare them better and was embarrassed. In 1982 and 1983, at AA Pioneer, we finished two great seasons, 7 and 2 in 1982 and 8 and 1 in 1983. Two of the toughest players we had on those teams were twin brothers Bob and Rick Stites.

They both started both their junior and senior years at inside linebacker. They were solid, coachable, and aggressive players, but more than all, they were passionate competitors. They competed every day in practice like it was a game and got mad at their teammates if they didn't compete with the same level of intensity. In 1983, we played at Monroe High School during their homecoming weekend. The band was playing before the game; fireworks were going off right after the "Star-Spangled Banner" was played, and our team was getting more fired up than the Monroe Trojan team. It was a tough close game that Pioneer won, 9–8, but what I remember most was the effort that Bob Stites demonstrated while he was hurt during the game. He would hobble off the field and then hobble back on the field, repeatedly until the game ended. Nobody was going to keep him off the field. We had a great trainer in Ms. Lorin Cartright, that would later become the AD at Pioneer. She did a good job of making sure there was nothing serious, but today's player and in today's game, he would not have gone back in the game. They both walked on at the University of Michigan to play football under Bo Schembechler and later earned a scholarship with their hard work and tenacity. They actually brought to U of M, at that time, the concept of communicating about offensive guards pulling across the center for traps and counters. We had taught them that at AA Pioneer High School, and the Michigan coaches liked the idea and used it at the college level.

The Stites brothers were responsible for that teaching technique sat U of M. That passion that they showed is why we were successful as a team, but more importantly, that same passion has propelled both Bob and Rick in day-to-day life as businessmen.

They own and run Stites Financial here in Ann Arbor, Michigan, and do a great job with the families' finances. Again the nice part of coaching is that thirty-three years later, we're still friends. They handle my finances, we have competed in handball, racquetball, and tennis, and communicate often. There are many young men like Bob and Rick that I've had the pleasure of interacting with over the years, and for that, I am highly grateful. Getting a phone call last summer from John Wacker in Hawaii, listening as he told me about his wife and family and even more grateful for the comments he made when he told me how I've impacted his life as a coach and teacher. He and his wife run marathons and exciting runs in Hawaii, through water and rough terrain. Currently I work part-time at the M Den, at Briarwood Mall, in Ann Arbor, Michigan. We have the best manager in Wendy Roberts; she is pleasant yet extremely effective at setting a standard of excellence at the M Den. I have had many good supervisors over the years, principals, head coaches, athletic directors, and managers in many other jobs. I just mentioned one in Ms. Lorin Cartright at Pioneer High School. Lorin was professional in every way, both as an educator, head trainer, and as an athletic director and administrator. I would also consider her a good friend and confidant. At the M Den, I work with both Bob and Rick's daughters, which is also a blessing to work with family members of two former football players. Both of them are bright young ladies who act as closers at the end of the shift and are students, one in high school and one in college. Wendy is one of the most encouraging managers, with a bright smile and hardworking example to her employees. Despite being in charge, she demonstrates leadership by doing the difficult menial tasks that all the rest of us have to do. Humility is what I believe to be the core of great leadership. It is easy to work for someone who is humble in their approach rather than dictatorial and heatedly dogmatic about the way they want things done. She manifests a servant's attitude while maintaining an extremely proficient working environment and professional knowledge necessary to run an enterprise like the M Den.

I've had the pleasure of working with several former students and student athletes that I have taught or coached when they were younger. Many former players, parents, students, fellow teachers, and other people that I had the good fortune to have met over the years come into the M Den to shop and say hello. I love to greet former students and players, while still maintaining my responsibilities and integrity as an employee. I also enjoy helping people pick out their apparel at the store and practice a good sales approach with them. To give an example, last Christmas, a young man came into the store, and I was in the back section working. He walked over and said, "Are you Coach Test?" I responded yes. He said, "Do you remember me? I played football for you at Pioneer in 1982."

Embarrassed that I did not remember who he was, I smiled and said, "Can you help me with the name?"

He said, "I'm Andy Raeder." And immediately I recognized him and told him his high school jersey number—83—and that he played outside linebacker.

He said, "You do remember me."

However, sometimes it is difficult to recognize someone you have not seen for over thirty years, or students that I had in grade school when they were ten, eleven, or twelve, and now they are in their twenties or thirties. In those years, they have matured from little boys and girls to young ladies and men. So sometimes, I just need to look at them and smile and say, "Please forgive me, can you remind me of what your name is?"

PITT IS IT!

My decision of what college to attend was finalized. So in August of 1973, I headed to Pittsburgh as a student athlete. For the first month, my roommate was from Miami, Florida—Charles, a.k.a. Chucky Cool. Charles was about 6'4" and weighed approximately 235; he was built like a Greek god and could literally run like the wind.

The first day I met him in our room in tower A, he pulled a piece out of his footlocker.

Charles was one of the nicest easygoing guys I've ever met, but being from Miami, he was trying to come across as a tough guy, which he really wasn't. The coaches tried their hardest to get Charles to start first as an inside linebacker, then an outside linebacker, then a tight end, and finally the offensive line. Try as they might, he never started, but to look at them, you would've thought he was ready for the NFL. Truth be told, Charles really wasn't a football player but a great guy.

When we went away to camp in the fall in Johnstown, Pennsylvania, a lot of players were sitting around in the cafeteria late at night, with music going; it was the disco era. Chucky Cool was sitting near me. Several of the bigger white linemen said to Chucky, "Hey, man, show us some dance moves." Charles motioned with this thumb toward me and said, "Ask Test, he's the one with all the moves. He's from the Motown." Charles knew this because we were roommates. So I showed them a few steps on the cafeteria floor.

Freshman camp in Johnstown was a bear. Midweek, I had lost my playbook and had to run extra after every practice—after we had already run. Needless to say, I was exhausted, but I hung in there. At night, the crickets were so loud they sounded like giant buzz saws in the night air. But we were so tired sleep came easy.

While being recruited during my recruiting trip, Coach Johnny Majors (former All-American from Tennessee and runner up to the Heisman award 1956, the year Paul Hornung won it) announced at dinner that Pitt had just signed Anthony Dorsett to a scholarship, to play football at Pitt. The seven or eight players at our table just kind of looked at one another and said who's that, why is he so special? During the first scrimmage at Johnstown, quarterback Billy Daniels, threw a little screen in the flat to Tony Dorsett; Tony took the pass, made a few moves, cut back across the field, and ran about eighty yards for a touchdown. Then everybody knew why Tony Dorsett was so special. He was very special, initially holding several collegiate rushing records, including career yardage of over six thousand yards. His senior year, he was Heisman Trophy winner, and Pitt won its first national championship in decades. Then he went on to play for the Dallas Cowboys and made the NFL Hall of Fame. He still holds the longest rushing touchdown on Monday Night Football, when he rushed ninety-nine yards for a touchdown. Man, he was fast. He was not real big; he was about six feet, 185. But he could run like the wind; that's why they called him Hawk in Pittsburgh. Presently he's having some issues with head trauma. I pray he is okay.

Left to Right: Ron Medley #42 W.R, Paul Test #31 D.B.

Ron Medleys wedding, Pittsburgh Panther W.R. #42, Paul, Donna, Ron, Norma (sister)

MOTOWN EXPRESS

As a freshman, we were on our way to Connecticut to play Milford Military Academy with the JV squad. While in the bus, a lot of players were resting or sleeping. I decided to start singing an old Motown song by the Temptations called "My Girl." When I started to sing the song, thinking some players might be annoyed, no one complained or asked me to be quiet. Instead one teammate, Ron Medley, decided to join in. We harmonized pretty well together, so well that the players asked for another song. So we busted out with "Since I Lost My Baby." Ron ended up being my best friend, and to this day, we still communicate regularly. He lived in Pittsburgh for thirty-plus years until finally moving to the Orlando, Florida, area where his son lives. Ron asked me to be the best man at his wedding and to be the godfather of his second son, Matthew Medley. Ron grew up in Madison, Virginia, a small country town that I used to joke about with Ron, but if you blink your eyes, you would miss the town. Ron had a heart of gold, one of the nicest guys you'd ever want to meet. He married a nurse from Pitt named Donna, and had four children. Mario played football at Kent State, about 6'7". Matthew, who I watched play in high school in Pittsburgh at Shadyside Academy, where Ron was a football coach. He has two daughters, Maria and Malanie.

Ron has come out to Ann Arbor, Michigan, to visit a couple of times. In college, Ron was about 6'3", 185 pounds. Now he is still 6'3", but he weighs about 250; so instead of being a wide receiver like he was, he would probably be a tight end or guard. That's just teasing him; he was a great athlete and still is. He used to tease me after a JV game about making twenty-two unassisted tackles, which in one JV game, I did. He's a great friend as well as a godly man. I'll come back to that present-day friendship at a later time.

My freshman year, I met a young lady. She attended Carlow College in Pittsburgh. We met at a dance on campus while she was with a friend, Liz, and my teammate John from the Detroit area was with me. John was attracted to Liz, and I took a liking to her friend, so we dated for a while. She had gone to Monroeville High School, and her father was a very prominent businessman in Pittsburgh and chairman of the board. Her family were very hospitable and generous to me. I was invited to their chalet in the Poconos for Easter dinner. I was always very respectful of their daughter, and it's a good thing I was, because the family, or *famiglia*, had a reputation that went way back. Nowadays you can look online regarding the demise of the brothers in 1930s. Back then, I had to go to the library and look on microfilm to read about it. I have nothing but love and respect for the family. One night years later, while I was sleeping with my wife, Pamela, the phone rang, and it was her calling on our phone. Our phone at the time was unlisted, but she got the phone number anyway—she had connections. The next day, I called her back and said, "You can't be calling my house late at night. I'm married. You wouldn't put up with that if you were my wife, how do you think my wife feels?" She promised not to do it again and did not. Sadly, she had called because she was sick with cancer, and she died shortly thereafter. I pray that she's with the Lord.

Just to give you an idea of the prestige that her family had, the name of the street they live on was the same as her first name, and the street behind that was her last name. One of her classmates from Monroeville High School was a teammate of mine at Pitt; his name was Marc, a QB. He said, "You better be careful with her. Boys in high school ended up getting hurt if they weren't careful with her."

I said to him, "I'll be fine. I treat her with a great deal of respect." And I did. She was an Italian girl from a very nice Italian family.

As I have said previously, my freshman year was very difficult, especially the second semester after my father passed away in January, January 25, 1974, at the young age of sixty. As I write this now, I am sixty years young, and it feels very young. I guess age is all relative to how you feel and where you're at in life.

As the second semester proceeded, I began to make some poor choices. I wasn't going to class regularly. Ron Medley, my good friend, and Bobby Hutton, starting fullback his junior and senior year, did a lot of blocking for Tony Dorsett. We went to downtown Pittsburgh, and I bought a leather coat and a black-and-white pinstripe suit; I guess I thought I was a gangster. I began to carry a half a pint of Kessler Whiskey in my coat pocket when I went to parties, dances, or to visit a girl.

Oakland, the section of town that the University of Pittsburgh is in, was a tough area in the 1970s. It didn't take much walking down Fifth Street or Forbes Avenue to get in a fight. One night late in the spring, John and I were walking to McDonald's when two guys stopped in front of John, just being punks to front him off. One of them took a swing at John, so I jumped in and began to fight with both of them. I managed to subdue the one guy while getting hit a few times in the back by the other guy. They really didn't want to fight; they just wanted to bully someone, so they took off, and it ended. John and I went to McDonald's and ate, then walked back to the dorms. When we were walking back, John apologized to me for not helping out. I said, "Forget about it, it's no big deal."

The thing is John was the kind of guy that would punch me in the arm jokingly and grin like it was funny. One night in the dorms, when he punched me in the arm, I got mad and said, "Don't do that again, or I'll kick your butt." It was just game playing, stuff you don't do when you're tough because you don't have to prove anything to anybody; when the time comes to react, you react. John was a well- to-do kid, not really a fighter. So most of the time, he was just trying to prove something to himself. But when it mattered on the street, he did nothing. He was a good guy, and he was also from the Detroit area, so we hung out occasionally back home.

I had a friend back in Dearborn who was very similar in that he would always start trouble when we were out, start mouthing off to someone, trying to start a fight, and then when the fight started, he was nowhere to be found. He eventually became a policeman in Dearborn. Now I really didn't go around trying to start fights or get in trouble. I've always tried to be friendly and have fun with people. But during this period of time, shortly after my father's passing, my attitude changed quite a bit, and although I didn't start trouble, I did my best to try and finish them.

I had always tried to treat people with kindness and compassion, but after my father's death, I really didn't care about being so gracious to others. Fortunately I did not do anything too crazy, although one night, I did get arrested and spent a night in jail; but someone was looking out for me, and the charges were dropped.

Toward the end of my freshman year, I was invited to a teammate's house in Indiana, Pennsylvania. Bill invited Marc and me to his home for the weekend. His father, a real gentleman, and his sister sat in the front seat of the car when we drove back to Bill's house. When we arrived at Bill's house, the three of us went out and partied till late at night.

Bill and Marc and I, along with Mark from Monroeville, became suitemate's our sophomore year at Pitt. John was supposed to be in our suite, but John transferred to Michigan State University our sophomore year. Bill had a good year starting at outside linebacker until he hurt his knee and was out for the season. Marc was a running back that saw little action, and the other Mark was a quarterback and also saw little action. I was playing on the JV team that still existed back then, doing quite well. After several good games, I was moved up to varsity, and Coach Jackie Sherrill worked with me on the punt block team. The most exciting time I had as a collegiate football player was during the Pittsburgh versus Penn State Game that was nationally televised in 1974. I dressed for the game. The game was played at Three Rivers Stadium in

Pittsburgh. I was really excited; many of my friends back home said, "I saw you on television." It was a good end to my sophomore season, and I felt as though the future held opportunity.

I attended church regularly at St. Paul's, just down the street from the campus, but I wasn't living a godly life. One night at a party, when I had been drinking, quarterback Matt Cavanaugh, a Youngstown native, invited me to attend a Fellowship of Christian Athletes meeting, a.k.a. the FCA, the next morning on Saturday. I told him I was busy and didn't have time for it. What a mistake that was for me; nothing would've been better then for me than to attend the meeting, but I did not. My priorities were not in order.

The good news was my sophomore year, my grades were improving, and I was going to class regularly like I should to get an education. One night in the early spring, at a Pittsburgh basketball game, I was sitting with Marc and Bill and many other Pittsburgh football players in the stands, and Marc began to yell racial obscenities at one of the officials who happened to be black. Needless to say, I was embarrassed and angry. Teammates of ours were sitting all around, both black and white, while he was making a fool of himself. When we got back to the suite, Bill's girlfriend was in our room with him, so I slept on the floor in the same room with Marc and his roommate. We had words regarding his comments at the basketball game. The next thing I know, we were fighting on the floor where I had been sleeping. Bill ran out of our room and grabbed me and was holding me from behind, while Marc hit me a few times. The next day, both of us had a black eye, and very little was said. I never could stand racism, especially from someone I considered a friend, so Marc and I never really became close friends again; although we did forgive each other and moved on.

I never did have a problem getting along with any of the black players on the team, although I did have a difficult time getting along with some of the white players on the team, especially those that were bigoted. I kept my distance from them but got into a few fights with several of them, usually much bigger than me. One was an offensive lineman that was about 260, that started to mouth off to me in the bathroom one night. I stood my ground and said, "If you want to fight, let's go." He walked away. Once in the locker room, another bigger linebacker hit me with a wooden bar as I was walking past his locker, so we got into until we were eventually pulled off of each other by some teammates. My good friend Ron Medley told me he didn't get involved because I was winning. Often they made racist comments that I did not want to tolerate. There will always be racism in the world because of the nature of man and because it is a sin, and sin will exist until our Lord returns. There will always be people that want to create hatred, chaos, and confusion, unfortunately.

Looking back at much of this, in retrospect, a lot of what went on was spiritual warfare, antagonistic behavior that I allowed myself to be a part of. I did not show enough self-control, and for that, I am sorry. I learned a lot from these experiences and have used that in dealing with the young people I've coached, as well as adults who have acted like fools. Beware of the anger of a righteous man. Don't take my kindness as a weakness; these are two of my favorite quotes. Forgiveness is a godly trait, but forgiveness does not mean stupidity; there is such a thing as righteous anger.

One evening, I was hitchhiking to a party with two girls from the dorms when a car pulled over and picked us up.

There was a young man driving the car, so I asked him where he was from. He responded, "I'm from the Detroit area."

I said, "What part of Detroit?" He said, "I'm from Dearborn."

"So where'd you go to school?" I asked. He said he was from Fordson High School, on the east side of Dearborn. I asked his name.

He said, "I'm Mario Papazzi."

I said, "I'm Paul Test, and I remember playing baseball with you in the summer in Dearborn."

He turned around, all excited, and said, "Ah, Paul, I remember you." The two girls just sat and listened to this banter, back and forth, laughing about the whole conversation. What a small world. Mario drove us to the party, and I invited him in, and we had a great time.

To quote Emerson, "He is only rich who owns the day." I felt like we owned the evening, and a good time was had by all. When I grew up in Dearborn, I had a lot of friends from the east side of Dearborn. We played baseball together in the summer, football in the fall, until they started the Dearborn Mustangs, then they played on their side of town. The Burkes, the Parises, Hattas, and a number of Italian families such as Papazzi.

One night at Levagood Park in Dearborn, I was hanging out with some friends, and one friend, whose nickname was Buddy, was being picked on by a bully, so I stepped in. Buddy really wasn't a fighter, so if you want to pick on someone, pick on me.

One of my friends in the background yelled, "Yeah, Test, kick his ass."

So the bully said to me, "Are you Denny Test?" (knowing his reputation). So I tried to decide whether I'd say, "Yes, I am," or "No, I am his brother." I decided for the latter. The bully backed down, and we hung out the rest of the night and eventually became good friends, so something positive actually came of that, of which I'm glad.

Pride and selfishness are often the ingredients to fighting and trouble. When one is only concerned about themselves and no one else around them, they are egotistical.

The best way that I think I can explain that is by discussing the concept of understanding. Understanding is to listen, know, or be tolerant of someone else's point of view. I have never purposely gone out of my way to start trouble. I have stepped in, especially when there was a need to help someone in danger. Maybe a story will help.

PERCEPTION

An executive called in to her office one day. Two employees were having a misunderstanding over a project they were working on. Inside her desk, she pulled out a little two-colored ball. One side of the ball was white; the other side was black. Holding the ball between the two employees, she asked, "What color is the ball?"

The person on her left quickly responded, "White."

The other employee who could only see the opposite side of the ball replied, "Black."

As the two employees stared at the ball from opposite sides, from their own angles, they could not agree on the color. The executive, while turning the ball, said, "Unless you understand each other's point of view, there will be no agreement on the color of the ball."

How many disagreements could be quickly resolved if we would take the time to look at both sides of the issue. Developing an awareness of the needs, feelings, and views of others is crucial to successful relationships. Although this story is as plain as black and white, it only makes sense when we understand that successful relationships do not begin with being understood as much as with understanding others.

The purpose of this story is not to purport situational ethics or to espouse views that there is no right or wrong, good or bad, but rather to make us aware that avoiding conflict is preferential when possible. I believe we are in a spiritual battle every day for our soul. Lust of the eyes, lust of the flesh, the pride of life, and the enemy, Satan the deceiver, the father of lies, are our daily enemies. Most conflict that we engage in is a result of our pride; pride says all that's important is me and my wants and my needs. I believe pride is the root of all evil. Conversely humility is a godly characteristic or virtue.

Let's consider the great deceiver, Satan, who said because of pride, "I will raise my throne to heaven I will raise my throne above the stars of the most high God, I will ascend above the heights of the clouds I will make myself like the most high God." You notice here he says he will rise above the stars of the most high God; he's not referring to the stars we look up to at night. He is making reference to God's angels. In other words, he is saying, "I am going to take over heaven. I will be God." Satan's sin is pride. He will no longer serve God but rather he wants to be served, and many, over the centuries, have chosen to do that. They have listened to his lies and chosen to follow him. In the garden, when Satan tempts Eve to eat of the fruit, he said to her, "You will be like God, knowing good and evil." And when the woman saw that the fruit was pleasing to the eyes, she ate it. Notice the lies, "You will be like God," because that is the very thing that he wants—to be God. Also that she would know good from evil; the truth is she already knew good and was about to experience evil.

Contrast this with the Christian experience of Jesus Christ in Gethsemane, when he says to his Father to "take this cup of suffering away," but quickly adds, "Not my will, but Thy will be done." His mother, Mary's, response to the angel Gabriel at the annunciation, when she said, "Be it done unto me according to Thy will." My will or Thy will, which will it be.

I am belaboring this point because today, many young people are deceived by the great deceiver, the devil. He is very real and very evil, and his purpose is to destroy you and me. He has made his choice, and that is hell. He has rejected God and heaven of his own free will; he has chosen to go to hell, a place of ultimate suffering and eternal darkness, a place of pain, pain, and more pain, and you are stuck there forever. One might ask, why does Satan and his fallen angels spend so much of their time tempting us to sin? Why do they care about us anyway? Quite a mystery, but we do know from Scripture that they are blinded by their lies and disregard for God's supremacy. If we're honest with ourselves, we can remember a time when we were angry with someone, and even though we were wrong all along, our pride and stupidity prevented us from seeing the truth. This is similar to the devil and his lies and his pride; he has never changed his mind, and he never will—he cannot. Some people say, why don't the demons just reconsider apologize and come over to our side? They cannot; they don't have to process their thoughts through brain cells like human beings. They don't have to process their thoughts; they see whatever they are looking at from every angle all at once. They don't have to try to figure out a problem or sleep on it. All they have to do is choose, and once they make a choice, it's forever, because they have complete conviction and understanding of the spiritual realm.

Satan was the most beautiful creature God created, and he knew that he owed God for his very existence, yet he made a purposeful and free choice to reject God. Because he is pure spirit, this decision is irrevocable. Because he rejected God, he rejected everything that God stands for: love, truth, and all that is good. Consequently he embraces evil, lies and darkness, eternal darkness, hell.

The person Satan hates is God, and he wants to hurt God. The problem is God can't be hurt in any conventional way, so he attempts to hurt that which most resembles God and was made in his image and likeness, human beings. That is, in fact, what they do and have tried to do since the beginning of time. Human beings are the target of the devil and his demons. What is of tremendous importance for each and every one of us is to know there is a great battle of good and evil going on right now for our souls. When we come to the end of our lives, and our bodies are separated from our souls, our acceptance or rejection of God will become forever, just like the angels and demons.

Now we have a free will to accept God and cooperate with his grace and mercy and love. The object of the devil and his demons is to influence our decision; they can't make it for us, but they can try to persuade us. One of the scariest things today is the proliferation on TV and in the media to propagate evil, witchcraft, sorcery, and tempt us in all of this demonic activity, and many young people are oblivious to the consequences.

The occult is very prevalent today.

One evening, my wife and I, in the late 1980s, had driven into Windsor, Ontario, Canada to have dinner at a nice restaurant called Casa Blanca. We had a great Italian meal, and we were speaking with our waiter. Our waiter asked us where we were from, and we told him Ann Arbor, Michigan. He replied that he loved A2 and all the activities available, and we agreed that it was an exciting city to live in with lots to do. He then proceeded to talk about occult places he visited, including in A2. He had first said that he really liked Turin, Italy, for the same reason—the occult and its practitioners. We became very cautious after this comment, and both of us began to just listen and look at each other, like, What the heck is he talking about? While I was listening to him, I noticed his face begin to distort, and it appeared as though all the skin had left his face, and it was like there was just a skeletal figure standing in front of us, talking. We asked for two espressos. While he went to get them, we both said at the same time, "Did you see that?" We both saw the same thing, and we were so upset that I paid the bill, and we walked out before he returned back to the table with the espressos. It was truly one of the weirdest experiences that I ever had in this regard. However, I think God allowed us to see that as a way of protecting us from an unexpected evil influence.

The media has the ability to propagate widespread falsehoods, lies, and create stories that have no validity. Oh, kind of like how the *Ann Arbor* News treated my resignation. Well, it, at least, was not the truth because my resignation as coach had nothing to do with the night of October 12, 2012. I had told two of my assistants in early September that I was going to resign the end of the season, and they would have the opportunity to apply for the position if they were interested, of which one of them was; that is the truth, not a falsehood. I had told the original reporters at the time that it had nothing to do with my resignation. Apparently they didn't believe me, and/or they didn't care what the truth was, and the current reporters either accept their colleagues lies or don't care.

Paul Test, Johnny Majors Head Coach at Pitt, Nate Bossary

Paul Test, Nate Bossary, Ron Medley, Pitt Alumni

Carlton Williamson, George Link, Paul Test, Ron Medley, Chris Zelleha (40 year reunion— N.C.A.A. Football National Champs 1976)

BAMBINO

Following my sophomore year in college, when I returned home, I dated a young lady from my high school that I had known slightly. She was having some trouble at home, and I wanted to help. One weekend, she left home to go stay with a friend. After one evening, I brought her back home to reconcile with her parents. It was a good opportunity for her and her parents to talk things over and amend their problems.

There was a lot of talking, crying, hugging, and warmth. She returned back home, and we continued to date throughout the summer. I had lost my resolve to stay chaste that I had as a high school student, and allowed the lust of the flesh to get the best of me. As a result, in the fall of my junior year, I got a call informing me that she was pregnant. Not knowing exactly what to do, I spoke to my brother, to a priest, and to her father. Father Zarrafa told me to take care of my responsibility but not to marry until the time when I knew that I loved her and wanted to marry her. Her father wanted us to get married and give the child a name—my name. My father was gone, and so I listened to her father and did as he suggested. I spoke with her, and we decided to get married in a civil wedding at the courthouse. We did not get married in the church, for which I'm glad because neither of us were ready for marriage. On January 5, 1975, we were married in the courthouse in Dearborn, and I returned to Pittsburgh to finish the second semester of my junior year. In retrospect, I was trying to make the best of a bad situation, one in which I had already made a bad choice. She remained at home with our daughter, Jennifer Lynn Test, while I finished out my junior year. I stayed pretty healthy during spring ball and looked forward to my senior year. I returned home in mid-April and worked as a security guard at the Fairlane Town Center, in Dearborn. Jennifer was a beautiful baby. I tried my best to be a good husband and father at the young age of twenty.

Paul, Jen (7 mos.) at Pitt

We traveled back to Pittsburgh together in the fall of 1976 and lived in the bottom portion of a rental home, while a nice Hispanic brother and sister lived above us. It was a very difficult time for both Jen's mother and me. In addition to being a football player, I took nineteen credit hours the first semester and twenty-two credit hours the second semester to enable me to graduate on time while still on scholarship. My football scholarship paid for full tuition, books, and housing. While living in the dorms and eating training table food for three years, eating at home with my family became challenging. My scholarship provided $200 per month for housing and food. Our rent was $180 per month, which left $20 per month for food.

When the football season ended, the Pittsburgh Panthers were 1976 NCAA National Champions in football. We defeated the University of Georgia in the Sugar Bowl on January 1, 1977. Tony Dorsett won the Heisman Trophy and went on to have a spectacular career with the Dallas Cowboys in the NFL and eventually being inducted into the NFL Hall of Fame. The sad news is today Tony suffers from head trauma and has a difficult time expressing himself. Going back to a reunion game in 2010, with Pittsburgh playing the University of Miami of Florida at Heinz Field in Pittsburgh, many of the 1976 team members met in the locker room before the game and had the opportunity to reacquaint with one another. We formed a tunnel for the current Panther team, and finally Tony Dorsett was introduced on the PA and the big screen, and the crowd went nuts because Tony is certainly a hometown favorite, having grown up in Aliquippa, Pennsylvania. But it is still sad to see the ramifications of four years of high school, four years of college, and twelve-plus years of professional football and their impact on Tony's health. My good friend Ron Medley, the wide receiver in the same class as Tony and me, has seen him since and commented that Tony did not seem like himself. I hope and pray that he is okay; he has meant so much to Pitt football. Tony Dorsett, in four years against Notre Dame, had close to 800 yards rushing, including 303 yards his junior season; and these were real good Notre Dame teams.

After the season ended, I got a job working as a doorman, a.k.a. bouncer, at a discotheque named the Razzberry Rhinoceros, located in Shadyside, a Pittsburgh locale. I worked there on Friday and Saturday nights, did my best to study, go to class, and be home with my family.

We managed to get by, although we were by no means eating high on the hog.

After having worked at the Razzberry Rhinoceros for several months, the manager/owner called me in to his office one evening and said, "I want you to find a reason not to allow blacks into our facility."

I said, "Pardon me, I can't do that. I won't do that, that's not right." The next night, while working, he called me again and said, "Paul, we're going to have to let you go." He was firing me. He said to me business was slow; we were not busy. That was a crock; there was a line halfway around the building every night that I worked, what nonsense. I was angry to say the least. First of all, there was no way in hell that I was going to follow his instructions about not letting blacks into the club. Many of the patrons were fellow football players, students, and even some of the coaching staff that were black. Friends of mine that I would not dream of not letting in to the club.

The owner's comments were to find a reason, like you don't have a collar, you have the wrong kind of shoes, or some other erroneous comment. So that night, I was fired. So I made a decision to keep a few bucks that were in my pocket; it was, at the time, a five-dollar cover charge. So I had a little bit of money in my pocket when I left, but I made a decision, based on his decision to fire me, for all the wrong reasons. The next day, I got a phone call from the manager saying, "You need to come in and talk with us. I think you have something that belongs to us."

I responded, "Before I come in, I think I'll call the *Pittsburgh Post-Gazette* and let them know why I got fired, because I was letting blacks into the Razzberry Rhinoceros. I think they'll like to know that from a student athlete at Pitt." He hung up! What a chump, a bigoted chump at that. I was wrong for not returning the money, but I made a decision at the time to help my family out financially, and I was wrong despite whatever the owner decided to do to me. I will make recompense by giving to the poor, soup kitchen, or rescue mission.

Maybe a story about an employee will help to emphasize true character.

CARPENTER

A young carpenter works for a very successful building contractor for many years.

One day, the contractor called the young carpenter into his office and said, "Son, I am putting you in charge of the next house we build. I want you to order all the materials and oversee the entire job from the ground up."

The young carpenter accepted the assignment with great enthusiasm and excitement. The next day, he went out to the building site and studied the blueprints, checked every measurement and every specification in detail. Suddenly he had a thought. *If I am in charge of this project, why don't I just cut a few corners here and there, order less expensive materials, and put the extra money in my pocket? Who would know the difference?* So the young carpenter followed through on his scheme. He ordered substandard lumber, inexpensive concrete, put in cheap wiring, and cut every corner that he could, yet when he filled out his report, he listed the purchase of better materials. When the house was finally finished, the contractor came out to the building site to see it.

"Young man," said the contractor, "you have done a magnificent job, and you have been such a good and faithful carpenter all these years, I have decided to show my gratitude by giving you this wonderful house that you have built, as a gift to you."

Laying the foundation of good character means never taking shortcuts but doing the right thing because it is the right thing to do.

The young man built a shoddy house to make money for himself while not realizing that the house was to be his. Would he have built the same house if he knew it was his? I doubt it.

Many of us take shortcuts in our character development, not realizing that it will affect the type of man or woman we will become. As a coach, when one is building a team, you do not take shortcuts to greatness, to competitiveness; or if you do, it will be reflected on game night by the way your team competes. The attention to detail in practice and the insistence of maximum effort by your players and your coaches will be the difference between greatness and mediocrity. I've always taught as a coach that when your substitutes get in the game that they compete with the same enthusiasm as a starter, because at practice, they work as hard as anyone else. Besides, any great team is only as good as its weakest link.

In the winter months, I worked as a referee for intramural basketball. Many of the games were between fraternities, and often there was a lot arguing and complaining about calls that were made by us, the officials. Since I was doing whatever I could to help facilitate family income, I stuck with it until the season ended. I kept the games under control and did not lose my cool during the arguments. I generally rode a bicycle to class, even in the winter with the snow, which was challenging at times.

Although I took twenty-two credit hours the second semester, some of the classes were easier than others and required less study time. One class I took called Human Sexuality was one such class. Some of the discussions in this class were ludicrous, even in 1977.

Was there any such thing as modesty, privacy, or morality? I guess not, at least not in that class. The professor would ask you to discuss your sexual behavior in front of the entire class. One class, two homosexual students spoke to the class about their behavior, telling us—the students—that we were missing out sexually if we did not experience their behavior. So we were missing out; thankfully I continue to miss out in this regard. I know that today, if one speaks out against this behavior, one is considered intolerant. My thought is I can interact and treat everyone kindly, without agreeing with their behavior.

Because we were very limited financially, I tried to find ways to have fun without spending a lot of money. We had a shopping cart that we pushed to the supermarket when we went grocery shopping. We pushed the cart home while walking from the supermarket to home. A lot of times, I would put Jennifer in the shopping cart and push her down the streets and in the back alley; she had a ball doing this. Some of my teammates came by the house occasionally and would also play with Jennifer. David and Randy came by a few times, and they came by the house to help us pack up when we moved back home. Randy Holloway played professional football for the Minnesota Vikings; he was about 6'6", real tall and rangy, but he could run, too, especially for a big guy. He was from Sharon, Pennsylvania. Dave was from Beaver Falls, the son of a dentist that played quite a bit as a senior. He was my roommate my junior year. I called him the brushinest, and he called me the sleepinest, because he was always brushing his teeth, and I was always sleeping in late. He also had a friend named Dan, who we both called the talkiness because he never stopped talking. His last name was Serb, but I called him Serbico, like Serpico the movie, so he called me Pablico, because my first name was Paul. May not make much sense, but I like nicknames. As a coach, we had many nicknames for the players and the coaches. As long as the nicknames did not convey any negative connotations.

Mom Tests' funeral, Audrey, Paul, Janine, Nicole, Sam, Wes, Dee Dee, Dennis, Neal

So it was time to travel back to Michigan—Mom, Dad, baby and all. I got my bachelor's degree with a major in speech communications and a minor in English, which I didn't know at the time, but those would be the first two subjects that I would teach as a teacher in 1978. Because our rent was up, I missed the graduation ceremonies. We had to leave before graduation, but my good friend Ron Medley told me that he heard my name and clapped for me. Though I did not walk across the stage, they still announced my name, Paul Arthur Fabian Test.

When we got back to Michigan, we rented an apartment in Garden City, Michigan, suburb of Detroit, with low rent, and we set up shop there. My first job was a cook at Amato's Italian restaurant in Detroit, just off Ford and Wyoming Roads. On one of my last days, I had made lunch for myself, a big plate of baked spaghetti with several ladles of sautéed mushrooms, meatballs, Italian sausage, and plenty of sauce. Grandma Amato asked me who that plate was for. I said, "That's my lunch."

She smiled and said, "That is way too much."

I only worked there for about a month before I got a job making more money at the Ford Brownstown assembly line, working afternoons from three to twelve. Fortunately I had this job lined up before I left Amato's. The job was very strenuous and physical. We lifted the bumper braces for pickup trucks, threw them on a hook going by overhead. There were usually three of us, so oftentimes one person would work like crazy for about fifteen minutes, throwing the bumper braces on the book, while the other two guys rested. We got a heckuva workout that way, but by the end of the night, we were all spent, full of sweat, and having gone through a dozen pair of gloves to protect our hands from the sharp metal of the bumpers. After working there for several months, I got my first real job as a quality control supervisor at the Dearborn Assembly Plant—*Ford Motor Company*. I wore a shirt and tie, just like I did for twelve years at Divine Child School. Now I knew nothing about cars, really. So as I walked up and down the assembly line, I would ask the man working there what they were doing, and they would tell me. It made a lot more sense to me to ask them rather than for me, as a young whippersnapper, to tell them what to do. I sensed that they really liked it, because it gave them a sense of pride in what they were doing.

My supervisor, Mr. Minor, liked me a lot, and as I walked down the line one day, he pointed to the production manager and said, "Test, that could be you in a few years." I looked at the production manager, who was standing near the final line, where cars were taken out of the factory to be loaded on two trucks or trains. The production manager was probably in his early to midforties but looked more like he was seventy, like he was about to pull his hair out, at least what was left of it. My quality control supervisor, I am sure, meant this as a compliment, but that's not how I took it. I never did like working in a factory. I had worked there about a year when things at home we're getting pretty bad.

My marriage was shaky at best, despite the fact that I was trying to be a good husband and a good father to my daughter. The limelight of college football was over, the glamour and excitement at the stadium was over. While I always considered marriage a vow until death do us part, my very young bride, I believe, went with the adage "until the thrill is gone do us part." Not a good recipe for making a marriage work. So after a short two-plus years of marriage, she asked to separate and continued living in our home in Detroit, while I moved into my mother's house. So while I continued to work and pay the bills to support my family, and being told by her that this was a temporary situation, she was fooling around with other men.

One night I was at our house, and about three o'clock in the morning, when some guy dropped her off out front. I had been holding our daughter, who was crying in our bedroom. I set her down and ran out the front door and got into a fight with the jerk that dropped her off. This was only the beginning of many rendezvous. So eventually after a lot of fighting, arguing, and praying, I was at a loss at thinking there was any remedy. Nothing good would come of my fighting with these idiots. I would either kill someone and go to jail, or get seriously hurt or killed myself—either way—for what purpose. The only positive understanding that surfaced was taking care of my daughter, Jennifer. It was obvious that this was not a temporary solution on her mother's part. She was only eighteen or nineteen years old and wanted out. In retrospect, I should have listened to the priest who said take care of your daughter/responsibilities, but don't get married until or unless you love her and want to get married.

One day, after more of the nonsense continued, I was in my home that I no longer lived in, and she was gone. On my knees, I prayed that God would direct me and help me, especially with my relationship with my daughter. I absolutely hated the fact that my family was being ripped apart. After praying, I opened the phonebook and dialed a Catholic school that was approximately three blocks away from my house. I spoke to the principal, and he told me they were looking for an English teacher that could also teach a few classes of religion. Now I wasn't living there anymore, but it was awfully close to my daughter. I drove up to the school St. Gemmas and interviewed with the principal. The school year had already started approximately two weeks ago. I told him I was a speech major with an English minor and attended Catholic school for twelve years. He hired me on interim basis for a month. After one week of working there, they hired me permanently for the year. Wow, what a blessing. Truly God was watching out for me. I was not certified as a teacher. I had never taught before, and the school year had already started; yet here was a job three blocks away that I truly loved, working with kids. I took about a 75 percent cut in pay from the Ford quality control job, and I went from about $35,000 a year to about $8,000, but if I had to do it over again, I would. Although my family situation was not good, many good things began to happen. I started coaching the Divine Child CYO football in the fall. My first year, we were 7 and 1. My second year, we were 8 and 0, and we were unscored upon, we didn't give up a touchdown all year, we didn't give up a point all year.

Pioneering A2 became my goal in 1980 when I received a call from Chuck Lori, head football coach at Ann Arbor Pioneer High School, from Coach Bill McCartney, at the University of Michigan. Chuck and I worked well together, Chuck orchestrating the offense and leading the team, while I coordinated the defense and addressed the soul of the team. I had received a call from Coach Mac, the defensive coordinator at the University of Michigan, telling me there was a teaching position at St. Francis School in Ann Arbor. I interviewed for the position and, still not having my certificate, was hired for the position of physical education teacher, with the stipulation that I would receive it as soon as possible. I had finished my certificate that summer while doing my student teaching at Cranbrook Institute, through Wayne State University, in what was known as the Horizons-Upward Bound program. The program at Cranbrook Institute did not end until the first week of two-a-days practices ended. So Chuck said to me, "We will not start practice that first week until you can get here," which ended up being 4:00 p.m. With Chuck willing to alter his practice times, I was eager and excited to get started.

The first year did not run as smoothly as we had hoped, the transition, and its speed bumps. We ended up 4 and 5, and that was not acceptable to Chuck Lori or myself. The team had issues that needed to be addressed. After losing a game at Bloomfield Hills Lasher, parents argued in the stands, calling one another names, including the N-word. Players on the ride back to Ann Arbor were fighting, and it tended to be racially motivated as well. When we arrived at home, Chuck lay on the table in the coaches' office and said, "What have I gotten into?"

We had a great nucleus of seniors coming back for the 1981 season, student athletes that were disciplined, smart, big, and athletic. They responded well to the coaching on the field and off the field. We ended the 1981 season 8 and 1, our only loss at the hands of Ypsilanti High School in overtime, when Steve Lawrence, who later attended Notre Dame University, kicked a field goal on fourth down. The Braves had run three plays in overtime and lost three yards but won the game with a field goal.

Defensively that season, we gave up a total of nineteen points, with the group led by inside linebacker Andy Moeller, Gary Moeller's son, who later captained the University of Michigan defense his senior year, along with Jim Harbaugh, the quarterback and current head football coach at the University of Michigan. The other thing is Jim Harbaugh would have been our starting quarterback at Pioneer High School in 1981 had his father Jack not taken a position at Stanford University as defensive coordinator. If Jim Harbaugh had been our quarterback, I'm sure we would've gone 9–0 and quite possibly been state champs.

Other members of that defense were John Wacker, who played at Ball State University and in the World Football League, Steve Wild, Kevin Raedar, Quint Jackson, Mark Wellman, Steve Woodruff, Camp Fellin, Dante Kimble, Derrick Lee, and free safety John Nairn, who played his college football at the University of Colorado, where he was recruited by head coach Bill McCartney. John started at the University of Colorado in their secondary and had a great career. Our offense was also impressive, with Tracy and Greg Parham in the backfield, along with Robbie Webster. One of the biggest offensive lines that we ever had included John McDowell and Ben Roush tackles, Jim Minnick at center, the current associate athletic director at the University of Michigan, Jerry Curby and Ed Kreske at the guards, and tight ends Darrell Randle

(ROO) and Bernard Paige; Derrek Lee often saw action as the only wide receiver, and the quarterback was Al Smith. It was a talented group but accomplished a lot on and off the field by establishing a work ethic, but more importantly, an ability to play as a team and to act like a team on and off the field.

I remember addressing the team during two-a-days and saying, "How can you be a team and care about your teammates—all of them— when you go in to the locker room, and all the white guys are in one section, and all the black guys are in another section? It doesn't work that way!"

With the foundation laid, Ann Arbor Pioneer dominated the 1980s in high school football. We were 7 and 2 in 1982, 8 and 1 in 1983, with our only loss in the opener against East Lansing, the eventual state runner-up Class A. In 1983, we missed the playoffs by one- hundredth of a percentage point, and we're disappointed in that, but it sent a message to the 1984 squad. The 1982–1983 defenses were led by inside linebackers Bob and Rick Stites, twin brothers who later walked on at the University of Michigan and earned scholarships from Bo Schembechler. One thing the Stites brothers took to the University of Michigan was an inside linebacker technique that taught the linebackers to yell pull, pull, pull when their guard pulled across the center. Coach Moeller incorporated this into future Wolverine defenses, something at Ann Arbor Pioneer we were quite proud of.

Deviating from football for a moment, I would like to talk momentarily about where my life was headed. In the early 1980s, when Coach Bill McCartney was still around, I attended an FCA prayer breakfast once a week in the mornings at a restaurant. Coach Mac had asked me and my former wife to attend dinner at his home.

We had barbecue in the backyard, and Coach Mac asked me a serious question, "If God wants you and your ex-wife to get back together, would you do it?"

I replied, "Yes, I would."

He said, "Well, that's what I'm going to pray for."

And I responded okay. I was very open to this, but it wasn't meant to be and did not happen. She went her way, and I went my way. I began to think about my faith as something that was important every day, all day, not just on Sunday morning. Attending the FCA meetings and beginning to read my Bible daily was changing my life and changing my heart from thinking only about what I wanted to listening to and following what my Lord and Savior Jesus Christ would have me do. I knew in my heart that had I been living that way in the past, I would not have been dealing with some of the problems that I was experiencing in the present; and reading Scripture became something real that addressed my thinking and my actions, not just something religious. Coach Mac was very instrumental in helping me change my thinking from selfish to others-centered. Fortunately I was able to invite players to the FCA meetings. One young man, in 1981, told me that it saved his life because he had considered ending it.

As exciting as the '81 season was, helping this young man and literally saving his life by the grace of God was of no comparison. This young man, Steve Wild, a great young man and a great football player, spoke to our 2012 Ann Arbor Pioneer football squad at our banquet and told them this entire story. I pray that if any young man reading this, or young woman troubled by anything, that they would ask God to protect their mind and heart and soul from the enemy and turn their lives over to Jesus Christ. The liar and deceiver, Satan, wants to destroy them; he has come to rob, steal, kill, and destroy, while Jesus Christ has come to bring life, abundant life. This is very real, and the choice is very real, but we do have a free will to choose what we want. I will quote Joshua, who said, "As for me and my house we will serve the Lord." Today many young kids think it is cute or funny to discuss Satan. Believe me, there is nothing funny about the deceiver wanting to destroy you mind, body, and soul and for all eternity. When we lose a loved one and pray for their eternal destiny, it is real and forever, not a momentary joke.

While I was single for over six years, I would pray at night, every night, that if I were to marry again, it would be to a woman of the

Word. God often works in strange ways, but this is how he brought my future wife and me together. It is a sad, exciting, and miraculous story.

While attending the FCA prayer breakfasts in the morning, I met a parent of one of my students at St. Francis School. His name was Pat Hoga, a wonderful godly man, great husband, and father to two beautiful children, Michael and Andrea, both of who attended St. Francis School. Pat had invited me over for dinner during the winter of 1981, close to Christmastime, and I accepted his invitation. His wife, Pamela, cooked a wonderful meal that I can still remember to this day. We began the meal with a Scripture reading and a prayer. I was later told that Pamela wanted to fix me up with one of her friends, but Pat didn't think that was a good idea, and she did not. I remember Andrea sitting in the family room, playing with some crayons and being real quiet, reserved, while Michael sat and talked with us at the table. I had a great time with the Hoga family.

When I arrived back at St. Francis School in the summer of 1982, I was told by some of the teaching staff that Pat Hoga had died in an accident that summer in July.

Shaken by the news, I immediately got on the phone and called Pamela to offer my condolences on the loss of her husband, Pat. She gave me a brief explanation of what had happened. I felt so bad for her, what a devastating blow. As it were, I had just received custody of my daughter, Jennifer Test. She would be attending second grade at St. Francis school that fall. This, too, was an amazing story because her mother, following nine weeks of prayer and fasting by my men's group, she decided to tell me one Saturday morning when I went to pick Jen up that she could no longer take care of her. Would I? I could not believe what was asked because I had been trying to get custody of Jennifer for almost two years. The harder I tried to get custody of her, the more difficult her mother became. When I stopped arguing with her about it and started to pray and fast, God took control of the situation and brought her to me. The Friday before that Saturday was the exact day that our nine weeks' fast ended. I was amazed but thankful for what God has done. The one thing I knew during my prayer was that if God was going to bring Jennifer to live with me, then I needed to get my life in order so that it would be the type of environment that was conducive for her growth. I was truly blessed that she came to live with me in Ann Arbor.

WOMAN OF THE WORD

Pam & Paul at Bob Stite's wedding, Mike Hoga, Pam Paul, Andrea,
Jennifer Pam & Paul wedding, Paul, Pam

I was coaching in the fall at Pioneer, so I had difficulty with Jennifer being cared for during that time. I would take her home from St. Francis on the way to practice, then head to Pioneer, which was close by. Occasionally a teacher from St. Francis would offer to watch her. Later Pamela Hoga and I were talking, and I asked her if Jennifer could come by a few days after school, and she said yes. Andrea Hoga was in Jen's class in second grade, so Pam offered to watch her a few days a week, which I was eternally grateful for. After several weeks of Pam's care, Jennifer asked me if we could stay to have dinner with them,

Pam, Andrea, and Mike. I said, "Jen, we cannot invite ourselves over. That is rude."

Andrea & Mike Dascola wedding, Andrea, Mike Dascola

Pam said, "Maybe sometime soon."

Gradually we became great friends. She was a smart godly woman that could cook great and was gorgeous too boot!

Pam, Paul, Jennifer, Andrea

Pam and Paul

Remember my prayer if I ever married again, it would be to a woman of the Word? She was certainly that and more. I was so elated that we grew close and that I was able to also parent Andrea, who, as young as she was, always viewed me as her dad or as she called me, Pop. Michael was older; however, we seemed to always get along well, and he is doing quite well still, in Fort Wayne, where he met his wife, Beth, and her two children, Eric and Lisa. They have been married close to twenty-five years.

In 1984, after losing a tough game to East Lansing High School at Pioneer, we went on an eleven-game winning streak and won the Class A state championship at the Silverdome in Pontiac, over perennial power Dearborn Fordson, 38–12.

At the time, this was the largest margin of victory in the Class A championship. We had great defense that season. The leading tackler was Robert (Bogie) Kirkland ILB, who did not start game 1 or 2; he entered the game at Highland Park at halftime, with us down by a touchdown. He played a great game, and Hollis Smith blocked a punt late, and we won a tough game against a good Highland Park team, coached by a great friend of mine and current associate director of the MHSAA, Nate Hampton. Our secondary was stellar with strong safety Hollis Smith, corner Mike Holt (a three-year starter), corner and great run support player David Hargrow, and All- State free safety Danny Vooletich, son of former U of M defensive coach Milan Vooletich. Our outside linebackers were Kelly Petrock and Devon Wilson; TNT were Aaron Boylan, Scott Everett, and Alec Jerome; while the ILBs were David McGinnis and Bogie Kirkland, both real quick and would hit you, along with Kyle Bischelli (now a lawyer) alternate, good tacklers but both weighed about 155 pounds, not big.

Offensively Cedric Gordon was the big playmaker at wideout, while RBs Jimmy Johnson(quick and shifty) and Brian Vooletich (a big back) carried the load. Ed Hesseltine was a precision QB that led the O, with an offensive line that improved each week due to Coach Robert Eanes and Chuck Lori, the head coach. TEs were Chris Kohl and Adam Burns/ John Pozwiak alternated. The O line consisted of Amaechi Uzogwi and Aaron Berlin (now a school principal) at tackles, Jeff Robinson at center (now an Ann Arbor policeman), guards were Brian Bailey and David Kreske; Cedric Gordon went on to play at Ferris State and set all-new receiving records for them and went on after to play in the World Football League. I was excited that we beat Fordson because I had grown up in Dearborn and knew many people from Fordson.

Pioneering A2 through the '80s with Chuck Lori will always be a great memory. I coordinated the defense and was the associate head coach at this time. Probably the best time I ever enjoyed as a coach because I did not have to deal with all the BS that a head coach has to deal with—fundraising, grades, discipline, and parental calls. We went on a twenty-two-game win streak into the 1985 season, with many returning starters from the '84 team. In 1984, we defeated Trenton, Flint Central with QB Jim Abbott and Terrence (too good) Green, who started at DePaul in basketball for four years. Jim Abbott played professional baseball as a pitcher despite the fact that he only had one hand, which in football, he still managed to take the snaps from center and throw the ball with wicked velocity. The week before we played Flint Central, he had thrown four to five touchdown passes, and his big target was Terrence Green. We were able to intercept six passes that Abbott threw. We showed our team defense the film from the week before our game and, to get them fired up showed how Green scored on a touchdown pass; but before going into the end zone, he stopped and tiptoed along the end zone line and then finally stepped over for a touchdown. He got penalized, but they had won by a large margin anyway. However, our defense got real fired up watching him hot dog at the goal line.

Another big motivator in that game, prior to its start, but Flint Central team, just next door to us in the locker room, was chanting, "We're not going home, were going to the dome. We're not going home, we're going to the dome," over and over again, for about seven to eight minutes, which seemed like an eternity. Our players didn't make a sound; they just sat and listened with their game face on and quietly made a decision, at that moment, who was really going to go to the dome! It was us, and we followed that semifinal game by beating Fordson in the Silverdome.

In 1985, we began the season with a big win over East Lansing, at East Lansing, when P. J. Bowman lit up the field with his running and his passing, and the defense shut them out. Late in the game, however, P. J. sustained a season-ending knee injury. P. J. went on to play basketball at the University of Illinois, in Champaign, Illinois, so I was grateful that he overcame the injury. Pioneer, however, lost him for the season in the next week. Chuck Lori turned tight end Adam Burns into our starting quarterback. Adam carried us through the twenty-two-game win streak and did a great job; he was more of a drop-back passer but had good athleticism. P. J., however, was extremely fast and a good passer that allowed us to run our option offense better than any quarterback we have had at Pioneer. In the quarterfinals, we beat Lansing Sexton, who, at the time, was number 1 in the state, and we were number 2. Sexton was an extremely athletic team, and beating them was quite satisfying; maybe too satisfying, because the following week, in the semifinal, we played a much less athletic Traverse City team on a snowy cold day that provided a good backdrop for the T-formation Trojans versus the much more athletic Pioneers from Ann Arbor. We scored late in the game to take the lead, then Traverse City returned the ensuing kickoff back to about our eight-yard line and managed to score the winning touchdown to win the game and break our twenty-two-game win streak. Traverse City went on to clobber Troy in the Class A championship.

Following the 1985 season, I was married to that woman of the Word, Pamela Test, my wife. She had been at the Silverdome in '84 and followed throughout the '85 season. We were married on December 27, 1985, at St. Francis Church in Ann Arbor. The reception took place downstairs at the Lord Fox, where friends and family of both Pam and mine came to celebrate with us. I was so grateful that God brought us together and that he had taken two bad situations—a spousal death and a broken relationship—and turned it in to something very positive— marriage and the blending of two families together, a threefold cord not easily broken, God, Pam, and me. We honeymooned for two weeks, first in Toronto, Canada, and secondly in Charlevoix, Michigan, up north. It was cold and snowy, and both destinations were wonderful. We stayed at the Four Seasons Hotel in Toronto, a beautiful city with great entertainment and fine dining. After a week in Toronto, we traveled all day through a snowstorm to get to Charlevoix. Driving was treacherous, but we made it to Foster Boat Works, where I carried my bride across the threshold of our apartment. The weather really didn't matter because we enjoyed being together inside and truly getting to know each other better. I did go jogging a few times in Charlevoix. Knowing how close we were to Traverse City, I was wearing my purple-and-white sweats, sending a message that there would be a payback to Traverse City in the future. We accomplished that in 1994 in Traverse City, when I was head coach, defeating them soundly despite many hometown calls. We had an outstanding time in both Toronto and Charlevoix during our honeymoon, picking up many mementos along the way. My wife, Pamela, is an antique dealer and knows a lot about antiques, which we managed to pick up along the way.

I wrote the following vow prior to our marriage:

> My Father in heaven, may I receive love, joy, peace, patience, kindness, goodness, faithfulness, gentleness, and self-control. I thank the Holy Spirit for imparting these gifts to me. I will use them to better my marriage relationship daily.
>
> My wife and I will maintain the spirit of peace in our home by denying self in meekness and humility, by forbearing one another in love, not getting into anger but displaying patience. As there is but one God, one faith, make the oneness Pam and I share grow daily. We've become one body, one spirit, as we unite together in love as your Word says. I forgive my wife as you have forgiven me, so must I forgive. Through forgiveness, your Holy Spirit can operate, as I make a decision to act in the fruits of the Holy Spirit that bind us together is a threefold cord, Jesus, Pam, and myself.
>
> Thank you, Lord, for the peace in our home, our love, and your Word that I have hid in my heart that I will not send against Thee. As for me and my house, we will serve the Lord!
> *Amen!*

Now I am far from perfect and have made plenty of mistakes over the years, but I strive to follow this vow each and every day. Forgiveness is a blessing, both from God and to our fellow man. And how can we say we love God, whom we cannot see, when we hate our fellow man, whom we can see? God sees all and knows all. If there is any person I have offended, I pray for their forgiveness. In the Lord's prayer, we pray, "Forgive us our sins as we forgive those who have sinned against us." The opposite of forgiveness is revenge or dispensing justice on the one who has wronged us. Although we can all appreciate the feelings of one who has been wronged and the desire to get even; however, it does not satisfy in the long run nor does it change what has happened in the past, so although I may still be angry, I choose to act in forgiveness, knowing that despite all the wrongs I've done, God has forgiven me, over and over and over again, not because I deserve it but because God loves us that much, His grace.

It's interesting that I began to live in Ann Arbor in the fall of 1979. I have become quite attached to the city over the years. Having been born in Youngstown, Ohio, having a father and uncle that graduated from the Ohio State University, and being indoctrinated early in life as a Buckeye, I found myself gradually becoming a Wolverine.

Having my high school football coach Bill McCartney and roommates and former high school teammates, such as Ron Vanderlinden from Divine Child who is currently an assistant at the Air Force Academy, in Colorado Springs, Colorado, and Jerry Meter, former player and defensive line coach at the University of Michigan, it was hard not to pull for the maize and blue.

One afternoon, as coach of the Pioneers, while getting a football signed by Coach Gary Moeller in his office, Desmond Howard walked in and signed the ball as well. Later that year, he won the Heisman Trophy, striking that pose in the end zone, and that football went for a lot of money at our spaghetti dinner at Ann Arbor Pioneer High School, our fundraiser. Later on in 1997, it was exciting to see Coach Lloyd Carr win the first national championship for Michigan in years, almost fifty years. I had had the pleasure of teaching his children at St. Francis School and learned a lot of secondary play from him in the early '80s. He was an extremely good football coach. In the current 2014–2015 seasons, the M Den has helped with the sale of wristbands for Coach

Carr's grandson, Jason's son, Chad Carr. "Chad Tough" is the axiom used to encourage prayers and hope for the life of Chad Carr.

So my loyalties as a fan have become "Go Blue." Living in A2 and working currently at the M Den at Briarwood, I enjoy seeing A2 get all fired up about the Wolverines. This season, I believe they will manifest the intensity that their head coach has. It has been exciting to see the success Drake Johnson has had at running back, and despite two serious ACL knee injuries, he is still vying for playing time, having displayed excellent vision, elusiveness, and speed at RB. I know I am bias regarding Drake, but I think he is still their best back.

Also I have an appreciation for my alma mater, the University of Pittsburgh, who has been on hard times of late; although the hiring of former defensive coordinator at Michigan State University Pat Narduzzi, a native of Youngstown, Ohio, should help Pitt improve immensely. They also have more returning underclassmen than most colleges in the country. Those athletes of exceptional talent are Tyler Boyd, WR, and James Conner, RB and Heisman-hopeful.

They opened with Youngstown State University for the 2015 season. They played in the tough ACC.

The University of Michigan had just hired Head Coach Jim Harbaugh, from the San Francisco 49ers, where he had success at both the college and professional levels.

Jim handed out ribbons at St. Francis School back in 1986 for the quarterback club at St. Francis School. A program that Kathy Green and I conducted for several years to encourage parental involvement with their children in throwing and catching at home. I had a picture over my desk at school for years, with Jim Harbaugh, Paul Jokish and Mike Hammerstein handing out ribbons to Ann Arbor St. Francis students in the gym.

Coach Jim Harbaugh will demand attention to detail and overall intensity at practice that would help Michigan to win a lot of the close game that they have lost the last several years. Really, there is not a huge difference in greatness and mediocrity at the college level. Jim is an intense man, and that intensity will show on the field game day. He will make the program special again.

Another story may help emphasize my point more fully about real impressions versus false impressions.

An amateur genealogical researcher discovered that his great- great- uncle, Remus Starr, a fellow lacking in character, was hanged for horse stealing and train robbery in Montana. The only known photograph of Remus shows him standing on the gallows. On the back of the picture is this inscription, "Remus Starr: horse thief, sent to Montana territorial prison 1885, escaped 1887, robbed the Montana flyer six times. Caught by Pinkerton detectives, convicted and hanged 1889." In a family history subsequently written by the researcher, Remus's picture is cropped, scanned in is an enlarged image, and edited with image-processing software so that all that is seen is a headshot. The accompanying biographical sketch is as follows:

> Remus Starr was a famous cowboy in the Montana territory. His business empire grew to include the acquisition of valuable equestrian assets and intimate dealings with the railroad. Beginning in 1883, he devoted several years of his life to service at a government facility, finally taking leave to resume his dealings with the railroad. In 1887, he was a key player in a vital investigation led by the renowned Pinkerton detective agency. In 1889, Remus passed away during an important civic function held in his honor when the platform upon which he was standing collapsed.

No matter how hard we spin the story, our character is what we develop day by day, in the little things that we do and say. Coach Bill McCartney, in the fall of 1997, held a gathering of men in Washington, DC, called Stand in the Gap. That day, a multitude of Christian men gathered, not to demonstrate strength nor political power but to display their spiritual poverty and failings to a holy God. In a spirit of humility, unity, and brokenness, they knelt to confess their sins. In 2 Chronicles

7:14, God says, "If my people who are called by my name will humble themselves and pray and seek my face and turn from their wicked ways then will I hear from heaven and forgive their sin and heal their land."

This was a powerful day in 1997 and, as predicted, was met with plenty of opposition. The USA is at a crossroads in terms of where it is headed as a nation. We can spin a different story and believe that all is well, but as renowned evangelist Billy Graham once said, "If God withholds judgment from America, He will owe Sodom and Gomorrah an apology." Does our character matter enough that you are willing to stand up for what is right, or do we merely say that it's all good, and there is no right or wrong? Like Remus Starr, we can try to spin the story anyway we want.

THE TRUTH

We live in a society today that tells us there is no truth. We can create our own truth. Jesus of Nazareth said, "I am the Truth, the Way and the Life and no man comes to the Father except through Him." Fr. John Ricardo says that Jesus is either Lord, lunatic, or liar. He cannot be just a prophet, as the Jews and Muslims believe, because he allowed himself to be worshipped and praised by humans and did not correct them when Thomas said, "My Lord and my God," or Peter said, "You are the Messiah the Son of the Living God." Rather Jesus said, "Blessed are you Simon Peter, for my Father in Heaven has revealed this to you." Hardly a correction or rebuke.

Islam teaches that Christ will return, but when he does, he will set Christians straight, letting them know that he is *not* really the Son of God? The Jews of his time killed him because he claimed to be God, so either he is, or he was lying about who he was—why? Or he was not all there mentally and deluded himself into thinking he was God? Would he have suffered and died for a lie or, if he was not sure of what he was doing, correct their misconception of him? In Scripture, even the demons know who Jesus is. They say to Jesus, "What have you to do with us, have you come to destroy us? I know who you are, the Holy One of God!" But Jesus said, "Be silent!" The people were amazed and said, "What kind of talk is this, He even commands the foul spirits and they come out." Even demons knew he's the Son of God!

I pray that all faiths—Judaism, Islam, and Christianity and others—can respect one another's differences and pray to have compassion for one another until one day we go before God and discover truth in its entirety. We will find out someday, and the Truth will be known. In the meantime, our society continues to move further away from principals of morality and compassion for our fellow man. In his Promise Keepers devotional, Coach Bill McCartney stated that the process for prayer as a godly man consisted of the acronym ACTS, or adoration, confession, thanksgiving, and supplication. Adoration means giving Jesus Christ both praise and worship and recognizing him as Lord of your life. Confession means admitting your sins, repenting, and reconciling.

Thanksgiving means expressing gratitude for all your blessings, and trust of God's provision. Supplication means bringing our requests before the Lord by petition and for others. These four steps will help guide your prayers and your purpose on this earth.

After all, we are all passing through.

In 1998, I was the head freshman football coach at Ann Arbor Huron High School.

We had a great group of freshmen, sixty-five players to be exact. However, Carl Tabb and his cousin, Jeff Jenkins, were superb players. We finished 8–0, playing only eight games at that time, having their first undefeated season at Huron. The following season, 1999, we were 8–1, losing only to Davison, near Flint, in a close contest (we, later in 2000, beat Davison to atone for that loss). Chuck Lori was my defensive coordinator with the frosh in 1999, and we had a ball working together again. Marcus Moore was a phenomenal TB that season, and our QB was another great football player, David Bloxam. After the 1999 season, Coach Paul Verska asked if I would coordinate the defense for him on the varsity. My only qualifications were to have my own assistants on defense and to two-platoon with our personnel.

We had over sixty kids on the team, so two-platooning was not a problem. He asked me to have Jim Dick coach the defensive line, and I said sure because Jim had been our freshman coach at Ann Arbor Pioneer, under Chuck Lori and myself. Jim and I met several times with Chuck Lori to review defensive line technique, alignments, stance, starts, hand placement, gap responsibility, and visual and pressured keys.

We had a lot of fun doing this in Chuck's backyard over the course of this spring, and summer, we were all on the same page. Entering into the 2000 season, Chris Westfall became the offense coordinator. Chris was a former offensive tackle that played for me at Pioneer in 1992. The defensive staff consisted of Jim Dick, D line; Andy Turner, ILBs; Mark Korzenowski, OLBs; and myself, defensive backs. We finished the season 9–2, with wins over four Flint schools, two blowouts at Bedford and Saline, and a playoff win over defending state champs Walled Lake Western, before succumbing to Plymouth Canton in a two-overtime game for the regional championship, 34–28.

We were a very junior-dominated team and returned many starters the following season in 2001. We also defeated Ann Arbor Pioneer in 2000. The year 2001 followed a very similar scenario, with two big blowouts of Saline and Bedford to start the season, four victories over Flint schools, a big blowout of Ann Arbor Pioneer, 38–7, a game in which I could still envision Chuck Lori bouncing down the sideline during our final touchdown drive with Jeff Jenkins running in for the final score. The *Ann Arbor News* that season had done an article on the coaching staff at both Huron and Pioneer, entitled "Color Blind," which could have several meanings. But their meaning was we didn't see purple and white or green and gold; what we saw were Ann Arbor student athletes. However, to think that the Pioneer versus Huron football game did not have a big "*" beside that date would be a mistake. When I coached at Pioneer, beating Huron always came first, and when I coached at Huron, beating Pioneer always came first.

In 2000 and 2001, the defense was nicknamed the Black Watch Defense. The idea came from my wife, an antique dealer who dealt with tartan plaids for Scottish clans. Black Watch was a military unit with the great history of being fearless in battle, and our defenses played as that type of unit. Black Watch plaid is a black-and-greenish type of plaid that complimented the green and gold of Huron. We also wore black socks as part of the unit. The 2001 season had many very good athletes on both sides of the ball.

On defense, we had a secondary consisting of Tommy Averett and Renard Strickland at safeties, and Keith Newman and David Bloxam at the corners. Bloxam may have been the best open-field tackler I ever coached. The outside linebackers were Tariq Dallal and Steve Rose. They complemented each other very well. Tariq may have been one of the most physical OLBs I ever coached, at 6'4" and at 230 pounds. He also had great speed.

The inside linebackers were cousins Jerrard Harrison and Ravon Ellis. Ravon weighed about 240, and Jerrard was about 230, by far the biggest inside linebackers I ever coached. The TNT consisted of tackles Lavon Gillespie and Chris Charkowski, with Trentman at noseguard. Both tackles were about 6'3"–6'4" and weighed around 240, while Trentman, a former fullback for me at the freshman level, was very quick and about 200 pounds. I never had a defense that was any bigger than this group. Offensively we were just as talented or more so with cousins Tabb and Jenkins at the skilled positions.

In the key game that year that we should have won versus Chelsea, our starting center got hurt in the third quarter when we were up 14–7 and driving the ball on their end of the field. We put in a replacement, and the center quarterback exchange became a problem, that drive stalled, and a well-coached Chelsea team came back to score twice and defeat us 21–14. Then to end the season, we lost in the first round of the playoffs to Monroe on any very muddy, sloppy field. Certainly a sloppy field for both teams, but with the type of speed we had, it certainly hurt the River Rats.

Although the Huron team was extremely talented physically, it lacked several things, including being others-centered or putting my teammate before myself. Unselfishness was a character quality that was definitely lacking on that team. After one victory on a Saturday, when we were watching film, one of our star players left the viewing area to go outside and griped about not scoring the TD because the coach called the quarterback sneak instead of letting him score. Truly sad. I never witnessed this type of behavior on a great team. On a great team, individuals sacrifice their own glory for the good of the team. This did not exist on the Huron football team in 2001, or we would have won state championship with the talent we had. We were the number 1 team in the state for five weeks of the season until that loss to Chelsea. The Rat Attack led the area in total offense, and the Black Watch Defense led the area in total defense.

Something that Ann Arbor Huron football has not done since. In 2002, Huron had a great nucleus coming back, had a new coach, and we finished the season six and three, with three disappointing losses. Our first loss was to Lapeer West, 14–13, a game that all we had to do was take a knee, and it was over but we ran a play, fumbled, and Lapeer returned it for a TD, went for two, got it, and won the game. A very talented Saginaw team beat us; they were led by former Wolverines Lamar Woodley and Jerome Jackson, a RB. Woodley went on to play in the NFL for the Super Bowl champion Pittsburgh Steelers as well. We did clobber A2 Pioneer 30–0 at Pioneer during the season and lost a close game in the first round of the playoffs on the final play of the game, an exciting game with Pioneer to say the least. Ann Arbor Huron defeated Ann Arbor Pioneer three years in a row, which has not happened prior to 2000 and has not happened since.

The year 2002 was the last season Huron beat Pioneer. Soul food for the Ann Arbor football fan.

The usual suspects players that left a lasting impression on me and the Ann Arbor Community

In 1981, Steve Wild and Andy Moeller, played inside linebacker side by side. That team gave up a total of nineteen points all season, the best defense I ever saw short of my CYO team that was unscored upon in 1978. Andy went on to play at the University of Michigan and captain the 1986 team, along with current head coach at U of M, Jim Harbaugh. Steve Wild was a very fast and aggressive high school linebacker. As a senior student at Ann Arbor Pioneer, Steve was struggling with several issues, stemming from some classes he was taking that had him questioning all that he believed and was sure about. It was causing Steve to be depressed. I invited Steve to a prayer breakfast at Denny's restaurant in Ann Arbor. Steve attended the breakfast and listened to coaches and businessmen discuss their relationship with Jesus Christ, their Lord. He saw the compassion they expressed for one another in a wholesome way. Thirty-one years later, Steve spoke at our football banquet in 2012 to the team that had won the SEC Conference. He did a great job of communicating to these young men at the banquet some of the stress and worry that young people face in high school, popularity, the "in" crowd, conformity to the current morality, and a liberal educational format in the school itself that espouses situational ethics. This is a transitional time for most high school students trying to fit in and be accepted by their peers. Often the problem of divesting themselves from what they grew up with at home from all the nonsense that adolescents are experiencing. Worry and anxiety become commonplace for many.

Steve learned that there is someone who will never leave you nor forsake you in the person of Christ. He could cast his cares upon him because he cared about Steve and the rest of us as well.

This story expresses how troublesome worry can be.

A young man named Jason worked on a train crew as a mechanic. He was healthy, ambitious, and had many friends, but Jason was a notorious worrier. He worried about everything and usually feared the worst. One summer day, the train crew were informed that they could quit an hour early in honor of their foreman's birthday. The crew began packing up their tools and preparing to go home. Accidentally Jason was locked in the refrigeration boxcar. Realizing what happened, he shouted and pounded on the door, but no one noticed.

Jason began to worry, thinking, *If I don't get out of here, I'll freeze. Gosh, it's starting to get cold in here.* He found a rusty screw on the floor and began to etch words on the wall of the boxcar. He wrote, "It's so cold in here, my body is getting numb. These may be my last words." The next morning, the crew slid open the doors of the boxcar and found Jason lying unconscious on the floor. The crew rushed him to the hospital.

Later it was discovered that every physical sign showed that Jason had suffered from hypothermia. When the crew returned to the boxcar, they discovered that the refrigeration boxcar was inoperative, and the temperature inside indicated sixty-five degrees.

Jason's worry and fear had changed his physiology, and he had made himself sick through the power of his own thoughts.

Over 90 percent of the things we worry about never come to pass. To recognize this truth, write out a list of all the things you worried about this past year, and you will be reminded that most did not happen or were irrelevant. Worry is like sitting in a rocking chair; it gives you something to do but gets you nowhere. When you focus your mind on positive constructive thoughts when faced with adversity, you will soon discover a new or different approach toward your desired outcome.

SOUL FOOD

Be anxious over nothing but in all your ways continue to make your
wants and needs known to God and God's Peace which surpasses all
human understanding will garrison and mount guard over your mind
and heart in Christ Jesus!

In 1981, another player from Pioneer that was exceptional was John
Wacker, a high-energy, fun-loving guy that played with reckless
abandon. He was an OLB, at about 6'2", two hundred pounds, and
fast and aggressive. He received a scholarship to Ball State University,
where he played, and then played some professional ball in Europe. He
currently lives in Hawaii, where I would expect John to live because he
really enjoys life, and Hawaii is a great place to enjoy life. I have been
there three times and, each time, did not want to leave.

It is so far from the Mainland, though, that seeing family, children,
grandchildren becomes quite difficult.

In 1984, I had the pleasure of coaching a defensive secondary that
was second to none. Hollis Smith was our strong safety. Hollis played at
the University of Cincinnati. Free safety Dan Vooletich played at North
Carolina University (son of U of M coach Milan Vooletich). Mike Holt
was one corner, and he played at Columbia University for four seasons;
the other corner was David Hargrow, and he played baseball at Ferris
State University. All four were excellent tacklers, forcing the run game
hard from the outside while playing the pass with punishing hits. All

but Vooletich returned for the 1985 season, which was one reason we had a twenty-two-game winning streak. Show me a great secondary, and I'll show you the potential for a great defense. The biggest challenge in 1985 was losing our starting QB in the season opener at East Lansing; one of our best wins there ever. P. J. Bowman hurt his knee late in the game. Adam Burns stepped in and did a great job with keeping the offensive flow going forward, but P. J. was special, and we missed him a lot. P. J. played college basketball at the University of Illinois in Champagne, Illinois. Keith Arnold joined the 3H Club in the secondary, and we also lost our defensive captain in the Huron game, Mike Holt. Vince Wortman, a junior, stepped in and performed fantastically. Vince also saw some action at WR. His senior year, Vince had a great season and committed to the University of Cincinnati. He had received an offer from MSU but hesitated because he wanted to go to U of M, and he had received a call telling him Michigan wanted him. Being an Ann Arbor kid, his heart was here. He would later join my staff as a secondary coach and defensive coordinator in 2008–2012.

In 1986, we had another Vooletich, Brian at RB, who was a fantastic high school runner, blocker, and pass receiver. Brian received a scholarship to MSU, where he played safety. After beating Westland John Glenn in the 1985 playoffs, which was led by former U of M RB Tony Boles, we were upset in 1986 when Glenn completed an out and up on our corner late in the game. A drive to tie the game fell short by Pioneer and QB Lewis Andrews (a.k.a. ICE). Losing just 4 games in 3 seasons, 84–86, we began the 1987 season with a lot of new faces starting. Defensively we had a cumulative GPA of about 3.7, and it showed each week as we improved weekly. After losing our opener to East Lansing, we went on to win 7 straight before losing the final game to Huron, the first loss to the rats in 7 years. With a chance to ice the game late, we attempted a field goal that was blocked and run back by Chucky Phillips for a TD and a Huron victory. You can see the game on community access cable because they play it over and over during the fall and winter months on what is called High School Football Classics. My only thought is, why don't they play the 1987 state championship game versus Detroit Catholic Central that Pioneer won that year 3–0, to become Class A state champs? Truly a classic! By the way, Detroit CC beat Huron earlier in the season as well, 17– 6, and lost to East Lansing in week 2, 24–7, while we had already beat CC in week 2, 7–2. In 8 consecutive quarters, we shut out Detroit CC that had 4 Division I players on the team.

We also avenged our season-opening loss to East Lansing in week 1 by defeating them in the playoffs 14–7 in the regional final. We followed that with a 35–14 victory over 10–1, Davison in the Snow Bowl. A cold blistery night with several inches of snow on the ground. So we did beat both teams that Huron had lost to in the regular season, just to keep it all in perspective.

In 1988, we also lost our opener to East Lansing, and week 3, our first loss to Detroit CC before winning six straight games to finish the season. We gave up fifty-six points that year to East Lansing and DCC before allowing a total of twenty-six points the rest of the season. The key to all of that was a player by the name of Leon Eddins, who played OLB for us, was recovering from a serious knee injury he suffered playing basketball the year before. Leon was literally a man among boys. Big and strong and real fast, he totally blew up the Adrian offense that year at Adrian. We can only wish we had him the entire season, but we did not and missed the playoffs by percentage points. By the end of the season, we were playing superb football, defeating an undefeated Ypsilanti team in 1988, 13– 6, coached by Bill Kohn at Ypsilanti, and then defeating Detroit Mackenzie, coached by good friend Bob Dozier and led by NFL Hall of Famer and part of the Pittsburgh Steeler NFL championship team Jerome (the Bus) Bettis and their big lineman Gilbert Brown that was on the Green Bay Packers NFL championship team.

We shut them out 35–0 and held Bettis to under forty yards rushing. But without Eddins early in the year, we were building each week and improving each week. Years 1989, 1990, and 1991, we finished 7–2 each season, making the playoffs in 1989 and 1991. In 1990, we just missed the playoffs again by small percentage points. Chuck Lori was extremely frustrated in 1990, when just prior to the first game against our perennial opener, East Lansing, the principal came out to the offensive bus Chuck was on and took four of our best players off the bus. All of them were super players: Reggie Thomas, a TE; Curtis Reed, a WR; Reggie Harris, a RB; and Keva Curry, a transfer from down South. Chuck's face showed a broken spirit, and I knew he had had enough. Although we finished a good football season, he resigned at the end of the season. I was not chosen by the principal for the head coaching position initially because as he told me in his office, he had a person of color from Detroit that he was recommending. One of the committee members told me he had a problem with Test and his openness about his faith.

I asked the principal about this, and he said, "Now you know what a person of color has to deal with." So he was equivocating my faith with racial issues he had experienced. I had been associate head coach for eleven years at Pioneer and helped to win two state titles. After meeting with him, he decided to confirm my hiring as the new coach at Pioneer. We were 7–2 my first season and finished 9–3, losing the regional championship to Adrian and Al Romano. My remaining three seasons were average 5–4, 5–4, and below average 4–5. I was tired and frustrated with our lack of offensive improvement and decided to resign after the 1994 season ended. In 1992, we lost three close games before getting beaten badly in the finals to Huron, and we were not ready for them our cross-town rivals. This was the worst loss I experienced as a head coach. In 1993, we lost two games by three points, and one by six points, and were unable to generate a productive offense.

In 1994, we lost 7–0 to Detroit CC, a great team, and a good Howell team, 10–0, again producing little to no offense. Our only game that year we struggled badly was a 37–0 loss to Detroit Cass Tech, a game they scored with no time on the clock, already up 30–

0. I did not say one word to the Cass coach about the extra score; we needed to do a better job of coaching that year and did not. I took some time off to focus on my marriage and family. I took for granted all

my wife had done for me and the kids for so long, and I told her that. It was a good time to refocus and draw closer to her.

Pam would often put Scripture verses around the house to feed the soul; that was one thing about her I'll never forget. She was a wonderful mother to our children. She was the first up in the morning making breakfast for the kids and seeing them off to school, while I would pray with them each morning.

My *pride* could get in the way at times. Pride can be a problem for all of us when we allow it to be a problem.

First of all, pride speaks of itself. Pride seeks to have all the attention on itself. Pride cannot be quiet and listen attentively to someone else. Pride always tells you that I know as much as you do and probably more. Pride is only interested in itself.

One problem that I have with writing this book is it is about me and my life, but I do not want to focus only on egotistical accomplishments but on those I love and the relationships that I have been blessed with over the years and have developed from coaching and playing sports. As a football coach, pride can tell you that I already know all I need to know, so I don't need to keep on learning from others that know more than I do. Coaching high school football is really about the opportunity to impact young men's lives in a positive way. To encourage them as athletes, students, and especially as men of character.

After coaching the freshmen in 2007–2009 at Pioneer, I wrote the following:

> There's a little boy watching you, watching all the things you do,
> Some day when he grows up he wants to be just like you,
> He watches you catch and run, he feels the excitement, the fans the fun,
> There's a little boy listening to all the words you say,
> He may not understand them all, but he'll be like you some day,

He'll grow big and strong and tough and fast, one day soon he'll hope to be like you at last,

But time moves slow—so often seems—his ideas and dreams are all so grand—he's just a boy not nearly a man,

Still he follows you on a Friday Night performing with all your vigor and might,

Soon the game is over, "we won" says the boy, 100–0, the opponent did we destroy,

"100–0 wow what a game,"

the boys view of you will never be the same, You are his hero— you and this game!

Now he follows you out of the stadium with joy, he listens and watches and mimics this boy will one day soon follow your lead, your dress, your style, your manners, your deed, will he be a man that others respect,or a player, a fool, a criminal suspect,

Does it really matter the example you set?

Well consider your heroes, as a boy that you met,

or adults, or your parents who trained you and would pray, that you'd be a man of character, integrity you'd display, Time passes so fast that we didn't recognize or see,

that the little boy watching is really you and me!

We had gone 27–0 in three seasons, and I felt great but knew there was a lot more to what happened than just winning.

Winning was a by-product of the things we were trying to cultivate within the kids. One question I had asked the kids each season was, what are you willing to sacrifice for the good of the team? I told them this story:

There once was a blind girl who hated herself just because she was blind. She hated everyone except her boyfriend. He was always there for her. She said that if only she could see the world, she would marry her boyfriend. One day, someone donated a pair of eyes to her, and then she could see everything, including her boyfriend. Her boyfriend asked, "Now that you can see the world, will you marry me?" The girl was shocked when she saw that her boyfriend was blind, too, and she refused to marry him.

Her boyfriend walked away in tears and later wrote a letter to her that stated, "My love, please just take good care of my eyes, my dear!"

Wow, he had given his *all*. Sacrificed his own well-being for her well-being—sacrificial love, agape in Greek.

Becoming a River Rat was a change but one I took seriously. In 1998, I had the cousins Tabb and Jenkins in the offensive backfield, two of the fastest kids in the state.

Carl could fly and was a very bright kid; he was our QB. Jeff was built solid and tougher than nails and would run over most players. He attacked the defense, and Carl could throw well enough to keep defense honest and could run like the wind when he got outside on boots and option plays. I called every male student in the middle schools that fed Huron and asked them to play football at A2 Huron, selling them on Huron football and building relationships. We were 8–0 in 1998, finishing the first undefeated season Huron ever had in football. I had so much fun I asked Chuck Lori to join us. In 1999, he was my defensive coordinator, and we finished 8–1, losing a close game to Davison, a game we later avenged at the varsity level in 2000, 37–13, and 2001, 35–0 with those same players.

In 1998 and 1999, we had over sixty-two players on the freshmen team. Most of those players stuck with us to the varsity. In 2015, Huron did not have a JV team but wanted to develop a football program at the school. You can't build a program if you don't start them in the younger levels. There already is no program at the middle school level; that was eliminated in 1990, when the ninth grade came to the high schools. It was cheaper to have soccer in middle school, and most kids entering ninth grade in A2 had not played organized football anymore. Each year I would ask players in ninth grade, "How many of you never played organized ball?" And three-quarters would raise their hands. It is now customary to play one sport, and that sport goes on all year long.

When I was a kid, we played football in the fall, basketball in the winter, and baseball and track in the spring and summer. If you were not athletic, you joined other sports less vigorous. Chuck Lori knew that not having middle school football would hurt Ann Arbor in the long run. There were also three high schools now, which bleeds the talent even more. Between three schools, many more sports, some that run year-round, and safety concerns football in Ann Arbor has been much more challenging to compete with the best. Saline has become a school of choice, which allows them to recruit players from all over the area; although it is a very good school and complex that they have. Two of my best sophomores transferred to Saline after I resigned in 2012. Tyronne Miller was All-SEC as a sophomore, and Cameron Cole was an up-and-coming star as well. We opened with Warren DeLaSalle and Birmingham Brother Rice in both 2011 and 2012. I thought it was good to prepare for the season that way, but one of those teams would have been plenty to start with.

You know you're going to play most of the parochial schools in the playoffs anyway.

In 2011, we had a RB that was special in Drake Johnson. He set records in track for running the high hurdles; he was very fast. He rushed for over 2,900 yards his senior year, up from 600 his junior year; quite an improvement. Our O line was extremely good, but when Drake was in the open, he was gone. I coached him as a freshman at Pioneer, where he ran for probably close to 3,000 yards as a freshman, but we did not have his accurate records. Our MVP that season was Travis Maezes, our FB, and occasionally we played him at strong safety; although we were a two-platoon system. As good as Drake was, Travis was even better as a freshman. He was tough and wanted the ball in a close game when things were difficult. The Ypsilanti Lincoln game was an example of that. Lincoln took an early lead with several TDs. Maezes said, "Coach, give me the ball." And I did. He ran at eighty yards for a TD, the first time he carried the ball on a FB sweep to the right. But that was just the start because he continued to crease the Lincoln defense over and over again, and we won the game in a come-from-behind fashion. We kept things simple at that level, and it paid off big-time, with the kids understanding what they were doing and why. By two-platooning, the kids played one side of the ball and got really good at their technique, week after week, doing the same thing in practice repetitiously. It also allowed them to be fresher and more resilient in the kicking game as well. Chuck Lori always said there are three parts to the game: offense, defense, and the kicking game. If you win two out of three, you'll more than likely win the game. Don't beat yourself up was also one of his big mantras. Travis went on to U of M, where he played baseball. He will likely get drafted into baseball in the Major Leagues.

Drake and Travis could also throw well, so we had a halfback pass and a fullback pass; both were effective as trick plays off our base- sweep plays. In one game, Drake's freshman season, we ran power left six times in a row, and each time, he scored. Three times he scored a TD and followed each TD with a two-point conversion. So to start the game, we were up 24–0 in the first quarter.

I know it is frosh level, but running a play effectively is more important than being tricky. The trickery only works well if it complements the base plays you run. Having a trick play or two for each game is also important, especially against good defenses that are well coached. The trick play should take advantage of something the defense does well or is a weakness to theirs. The reason we went 27–0 was we had a lot of depth, two-platooned, stayed fairly healthy (although we had some key injuries as well), had a great kicking game (i.e., no blocked punts, good coverage), and ran the opponents offense at the first defense so much that they knew it, as well as our opponent did, and had solid coaches at each position because we met in the off-season to teach our system.

My wife, Pamela, has always been a blessing to me, and I am grateful for her. She is an anchor, she is strong in character, well versed in Scripture, and lives it daily. She was and is a wonderful mother to our three children. She stays faithful when things are tough and trusts God to meet her needs and her family's needs. She is intelligent and keeps me on my toes with current issues and with family-related concerns. She has kept me focused on the Lord by her example, and I trust her with my very life. The last time the kids were around the table, I read this verse derived from Psalm 105:

How great is our God, and how I love to sing God's praises! "Whereas I am often frightened When I think of the future and confused and disturbed By the rapidly changing events about me, My heart is secured and made glad When I remember how God has cared for me throughout the past. When I was brought forth from my mother's womb, God's hand was upon me. Through parents and people who cared, God loved and sheltered me, And set me upon the course for my life. Through illness and accident My God has sustained me.

Around pitfalls and precipices God has safely led me, When I became rebellious and struck out on my own, God waited patiently for me to return. When I fell on my face in weakness and failure, God gently set me upon my feet again. God did not always prevent me from hurting myself, But God took me back to heal my wounds. Even out of the broken pieces of my defeats God created a vessel of beauty and usefulness. Through trials and errors, failures and successes, My God has cared for me. From infancy to adulthood, God has never let me go. God's love has led me or followed me, through The valleys of sorrow and the highlands of Joy, Through times of want and years of abundance. God has bridged impassable rivers, And moved impossible mountains. Sometimes through me sometimes in spite of me, God seeks to accomplish great purposes in my life. God has kept me through the stormy past; And will secure and guide me through the unknown future. I need never be afraid, no matter how uncertain The months or years ahead of me, How Great is my God, and how I love to sing God's praises!

I feel so refreshed when I read this because it reminds me that God is in control despite when I screw up or make mistakes in my life. His mercy endures forever, thank God.

Character is important, and as a teacher in Ann Arbor, I always tried to emphasize this in my class and on the football field. In teaching physical education, I always began class with a character quality word or a *life skill* word. I only took about three to four minutes to discuss it with the class but always applied the word to something we were doing in class or something that needed to be addressed with the class. It always followed our four to five-minute warm-up, which had all students—second grade and up—enter the gym walking, then jogging around the gym. After the laps, they did sit-ups, push-ups, and line jumps.

They then paired up to do cross-lateral activities with their partner. This also taught cooperation because they had to work together through this time. Cross laterality teaches coordination but more importantly, right brain and left brain coordination.

Studies have shown that cross laterality helps with reading comprehension and mental recall. It also requires and promotes a cooperative learning environment. I studied years ago that most minority students learned better in a cooperative learning environment than isolated or alone. So many issues were being addressed during this short time.

Back in 2001, I had a parent complain about having a character quality word in the gym. I was crossing the line between church and state? We met with the principal, Pat Manley, who was very supportive of me but listened to the complaint fully. The parent was not happy with the CQ words. After listening and talking with the parent, I asked, "What word or definition is it that bothers you?"

To which he replied, "It is not the words or definitions that I am concerned with, it is you."

I knew he was referencing my faith, so at this point, I responded, "I am a Christian, and I make *no* apologies for that, and that will never change."

Even today, if ISIS takes over our country, it would not change. I did change the word to life skill word because that is part of our curriculum in A2. Pat, my principal, was supportive and knew that I was not abusing any of these learning opportunities. The greatest part of this whole story was in the long run, the family and I got along fine, and the children were great. And before their last child left grade school, he thanked me for teaching his children. One thing that they probably learned, too, was at the middle school and high school levels, there is a lot of craziness that goes on; not a whole lot of discipline, which creates a good learning environment. If a teacher spends most of their day putting out fires, then a lot of learning goes by the wayside. When I taught at A2 Saint Francis, usually more learning went on in a day than often took place in a week at some of our public grade schools. Disciplinary issues and troubleshooting were often the cause of this. I never allowed this in my class.

My first year at Thurston Elementary, while I was teaching, two fifth graders walked in late and were talking loudly, interrupting my class while I was preparing them for activities. I said, "Get back out of the gym and come in here quietly!"

One said to me, "You are only saying that because we are black."

I said, "I don't care if you are chartreuse. Get out that door and come in quietly."

They responded and obeyed. All they were really doing was testing me to see if I would cower to their nonsense, and then they could get away with whatever they wanted to. That would never happen. We spent about ten minutes that day discussing that character is not a racial issue but an internal issue of behavior and attitude. I quoted Dr. King's speech regarding race, "I dream of the day when my children will not be judged by the color of their skin, but by the content of their character." It was their character that I was addressing, and it was unacceptable how they disrespected me and their classmates by being obnoxious in their entry. In essence, they were just being rude.

Discipline on the football field was just as important as in the classroom. Now I am not talking about being a hard-ass all the time with kids but rather just being real and caring. If you care, you will create an atmosphere of respect, compassion, and discipline.

"Kids don't care how much you know until they know how much you care." This is one of my favorite sayings. In the classroom or gym, I would stand close to those students that are challenging as they entered the room or gymnasium. I would find something positive to say or do to those students as they entered. It might just be a high five or "Hey, man, you got it going today." To be *proactive* was extremely important because the difficult student is going to get your attention one way or the other. I would rather it be positive than negative correction or discipline. That said, there are times for consequences for inappropriate behavior, and the consequence should coincide with the misbehavior.

As a coach, I never kicked a kid off the team; I did not believe in doing that. There were times when players quit, but that was their choice if they did not want to adhere to the acceptable standards. If they were strictly all about themselves, selfish, and not the good of the team, they would leave on their own volition. We always said yes, sir, no, sir, on and off the field because it fostered an environment of respect that went both ways. I never cussed kids out or tried to degrade them. I really enjoyed giving them praise when they deserved it, and they enjoyed hearing it. If I accidentally said any inappropriate word on the field, I would run after practice, just like the players, to remind them that I was trying to set an example for them. That I'm human and make mistakes too. It all revolves around standards of excellence that are established to create an environment of success and winning.

A short story to emphasize excellence over mediocrity or being "pretty good."

Pretty Good

There once was a pretty good student who sat in a pretty good class and was taught by a pretty good teacher Who always let pretty good pass. He wasn't terrific at reading, He wasn't a whiz-bang at Math, But for him education was leading straight down a pretty good path. He didn't find school too exciting,

But he wanted to do pretty well,And he did have some trouble with writing, And nobody had taught him to spell.When doing arithmetic problems, pretty good was regarded as fine,five plus five didn't always add up to be ten, A pretty good answer was nine!The pretty good class that he sat in, was part of a pretty good school,And the student was not an exception, On the contrary, he was the rule.The pretty good school that he went to, Was there in a pretty good town,And nobody there seemed to notice, He could not tell a verb from a noun. The pretty good student in fact was, part of a pretty good mob,And the first time he knew what he lacked was when he looked for a pretty good job.It was then, when sought a position,he discovered that life could be tough,And he soon had a sneaky suspicion, pretty good might not be good enough. The pretty good town in our story,was part of a pretty good state, which had pretty good aspirations, and prayed for a pretty good fate. There once was a pretty good nation, pretty proud of the greatness it had, which learned much too late,If you want to be great,pretty good is in fact pretty bad!

If our country is going to be great again, we need to keep our standards high, not lower them for anyone. Coach Joe Paterno spoke at a spring football clinic at Penn State University in the spring of 2010, in State College, Pennsylvania.

I went to visit my former high school teammate and PSU inside linebacker, Coach Ron Vanderlinden.

He had been there since 2002 and was the only coach that remained after the firing of Coach Paterno and the Jerry Sandusky incident/ scandal that rocked the nation. I was saddened to see a great coach and man destroyed by the losing of his job and prestige after sixty-plus years of coaching. Coach Paterno said that if anyone can reach our young people today, it is high school coaches that model the standards of excellence that our country was based on.

Woman of the Word, that is what I refer to my wife as, as I have said. She was the daughter of a minister. Her father built and ran a rescue mission in Indiana. Charles Dickinson was his name, and there is a plaque outside the mission that is dedicated to him. His motto was "Soup, Soap (a shower), and Salvation" (coming to know Jesus Christ as your Savior). He helped many, many people over the years. Pamela attended a Christian college in Indiana. She taught kindergarten in Indiana, living in a small town—Shelbyville, Indiana— before moving to Ann Arbor in the '70s. She and her now-deceased husband, Patrick, had a son—Michael—at that time in Indiana. I met Michael at A2 Saint Francis School when he was in about fourth grade. They had Andrea in December of 1975 in Indiana. After Pat's untimely death in 1982, Pam's faith kept her strong despite the loss of a loved one. She trusted God to meet her needs. She wasn't out bar-hopping or going to pick up joints. God brought a young man to her door, and that young man was me. I feel blessed that we became friends first and had a healthy respect for each other. Rather than a romantic interest first, that developed over time as we got to know each other better. We often laughed a lot while she made dinner, and I occasionally helped out. I mowed her lawn and did other odd jobs that she wasn't into. I would also sing to her from time to time, and that, too, was the beginning of romance.

The first time I kissed Pamela at her home, I felt terrible, like I was not being honorable. Pat had been my friend, and I felt guilty for kissing her. Pam said in response to my reaction, "What do you want me to do, go sit in the corner and cry my life away?" A good response, to say the least. Henry Van Dyke wrote the following, "Time is too slow for those who wait, too swift for those who fear, too long for those who grieve, too short for those who rejoice, But for those who love, Time is an Eternity!:

She had grieved, and it was time to move forward and rejoice that God had brought us together. Ecclesiastes chapter 3 also reminds us:

There is a time for everything, and a season for every activity under heaven. A time to be born and a time to die, a time to plant and a time to uproot, a time to oil and a time to heal, a time to tear down and a time to build, a time to weep and a time to laugh, a time to mourn and a time to dance, a time to scatter and a time to gather in, a time to embrace and a time to refrain, a time to search and a time to stop, a time to keep and a time to throw away, a time to tear and a time to mend, a time to be silent and a time to speak, a time to love and a time to hate, a time for war and a time for peace.

I know that everything God does will endure forever!

As you gauge how much time you want to invest in priorities that matter most, rest assured that "no one gets out alive!" So although many things are important, such as work, school, study, business, and cleaning, the only thing that will last is what is done for eternity, spiritual. My favorite scripture verse is from 2 Corinthians 4:18, "For we fix our attention not on what is seen, but what is unseen; for what is seen is temporary, (brief and fleeting) but the things that are unseen or invisible will last forever, are eternal, everlasting."

Faith, hope, and love are everlasting, but the greatest of these is love! Years ago, a friend of mine said that it is not that you are busy and not at home that frustrates your wife but the idea in her head that you would rather be somewhere else than with her.

Many of the hours I spent coaching or teaching or working to support my family were hours well spent from a wordily perspective of providence and care for my family. What I needed to work on more was letting my wife know or reassure her, there is no place I'd rather be than with her, even if she knew I had to be elsewhere. To miss a faculty meeting or skip a week of classes could cost me a job; that is practical, but letting the person you are married to know how much you love her and how much you miss her will help to compensate for the time you can't be there. With that said, when it comes time for our departure from this earth, few would say I should have spent more time at work. I doubt that will be said. I doubt that most people will wish they spent more time away from family. I think most people will wish they spent more time communing with God, whom they may be spending an eternity with depending on the choices and decisions they made here on earth. Focus on the family, an opportunity to enjoy family time, and meet the needs of each family member. Pamela was the preparer of our soul food.

The following is a letter I wrote to my staff in 2012. My goal was for our staff to promote the proper attitude with the student athletes that would be conducive for a winning environment, and it was:

Character is a rarity these days. Often we look at the leaders of our society and are disappointed at their lack of character. Contrast the character of a man that God describes with that of the world. The world tells us to look out for number one, myself, put our wants first and see the riches of this world. God tells us a lot about wisdom and instruction: The reward for Humility and reverence for god is riches and long life. Proverbs 22:19 Pride goes before destruction and a haughty spirit before a fall. Proverbs 16:18 There is way which seems right to man, but its end is the way of death and destruction.

Proverbs 16:25 & 14:12 Commit your work to the Lord and your plans will be established, or succeed, (for His purposes) Proverbs 16:3 The way (or ideas) of a fool is right in his own eyes, but a wise man listens to Godly advise. Proverbs 12:15 When pride comes then comes disgrace, but with Humility is wisdom. Proverbs 11:2 Trust in the Lord with all your heart and do not rely on your own understanding, but in all your ways (decisions) acknowledge Him and He will make your paths straight (guide your decisions). Be not wise in your own eyes, reverence God and turn away from evil.

Proverbs 3:5–7 I hope you receive this with an open mind and heart.

My prayer is that you will succeed in all you do and that all you do will give glory to God!

Sincerely, Coach Test

MR. TEST — He helped Pioneer win two state championships in 1984 and 1987 as the defensive coordinator under Huck Lori. Friday, athletic director Lorin Cartwright, right, presented Test with the Legacy Award at the Pioneer Booster Club's ninth annual Gala and Hall of Fame Induction Dinner at Weber's Inn. Angela J. Cesere | AnnArbor.com

Test returns to coach Pioneer football team

Paul, Lorin Cartwright A.D. / Ann Arbor Pioneer

Ann Arbor Pioneer football team 2012, Team prayer, standing: Kevin Perry, Tom Barbieri, Paul, Rolando Eccelston, Lorin Cartwright A.D.

The kids responded well to this leadership, which allowed us to be league champs and playoff contenders both seasons. To finish as well in 2012 as we did, despite losing our starting QB, FB/TE, three DBs, one of our best RBs, an ILB, and one lineman on defense was surprising. We defeated Saline in week 4, 7–6, despite having six turnovers.

We needed to develop our offense better than we did in 2012. The defense made weekly improvement despite all the injuries, while our offense did not. That was my responsibility, and I should have been more involved with the offense than I was. I have always tended to be more involved defensively than on the offense. In the future, I would spend more time preparing the defense in the off-season and take charge of the offense myself during the season. Again this was one of Chuck Lori's beliefs, that the head coach can control the game better on offense than on defense. I have found this to be true and would handle the offense in any future head coaching endeavors. As an assistant, I still prefer being a defensive coordinator.

In addition to the virtues listed on the previous page, the virtue of love is at the top of the list. Communicating to our teams that love for self, one another, and even our enemy can create in us a motivation that far transcends having a vengeful attitude toward one's opponent, classmate, fellow worker, or rival. I wrote this several years ago to convey the difference between love and lust. I read it at a banquet in 2007 or 2008, and a parent asked me for a copy. I did not have a copy then at the time, but I do now, and she can read this.

LOVE VERSUS LUST

Love is personal, lust is impersonal.

Love is concrete, focused on a particular object,

Lust is unfocussed, capable of fixing on almost any available object.

Love tends toward faithfulness,

Lust is a wanderer.

Love seeks stability,

Lust is short lived, mercurial or erratic.

Love is an affair of the mind and heart,

Lust is an affair of the hormones and emotions.

Love is a matter of giving,

Lust is a matter of taking.

Feelings change and are capricious, volatile, fickle, willful, whimsical and unpredictable;

But Loving Commitment, is a decision and an abiding reality.

Love, God's Love, does not insist on its own way, rather it rejoices in Truth.

Love is not selfish, conceited or puffed up with pride.

Love endures long and is patient and kind.

Love does not keep track of injustices done to it.

Love never fails or comes to an end,

Love lasts forever!

Which do you chose for your life?

Choose wisely!

The person that displayed love to me and our family more than anyone was my mother, Deniece M. Test, the Texas star. She taught us faith, but as St. Paul reminds us that faith is great and so is hope; but the greatest of these is love. She was always there for us even when things were difficult, especially when things were difficult. The most important concept that one considers when they lose a loved one is where will that individual spend eternity? If you believe that when your time is over, that you are done and all is gone, I feel sorry for you. How depressing to think that all we have lived for over the years and whatever legacy we left behind is of no importance whatsoever. My mother was always reminding us that God loves us, and if we pray to Him, we will experience His presence right here on earth, until that time when we leave this earth to be in his presence for eternity. Quoting St. Ambrose from early writings, "To continue living forever—endlessly—appears more like a curse than a gift." Death, admittedly, one would wish to postpone for as long as possible. But to live always, without end, this, all things considered, can only be monotonous, and ultimately unbearable. Death was not part of nature; it became part of nature. God did not decree death from the beginning; he prescribed it as a remedy. Human life, because of sin, began to experience the burdens of wretchedness in unremitting labor and unbearable sorrow. There had to be a limit to its evils; death had to restore what life had forfeited. Without the assistance of God's grace, unmerited favor, immortality is more of a burden than a blessing. Death is then no cause for mourning, but it is the cause for rejoicing because it is mankind's salvation. Do we fully understand what eternity is? I know I certainly do not. But I do know what St. John said in scripture, John 16:22, quoting Jesus, "I will see you again and your hearts will rejoice, and no one will take your joy away from you." That is reassuring to know that we will be in his presence and not in eternal torment, if we have accepted him as our Lord and Savior.

Unconditional love is what we are expressing here. God has offered to us an atonement for our sins and wrongs here on earth. Again a story may better help express this concept.

UNCONDITIONAL LOVE

The story is told of a soldier shown as finally coming home after having fought in the Vietnam War. He called his parents from San Francisco.

"Mom and Dad, I'm coming home at last, but I have favor to ask of you. I have a friend that I'd like to bring home with me."

"Sure, we would love to meet him."

"There is something that you should know about him," the son continued. "He was hurt pretty badly in the fighting. He stepped on a land mine and lost an arm and a leg. He has nowhere else to go, and I want him to come live with us."

"I'm sorry to hear that, son. Maybe we can help him find somewhere to live."

"No, Mom and Dad, I want him to live with us."

"Son," said the father, "you don't know what you are asking. Someone with such a handicap would be a terrible burden on us. We have our own lives to live, and we can't let something like this interfere with our lives. I think you should just come home and forget about this guy. He'll find a way to live on his own." At that point, the son hung up the phone. The parents heard nothing more from him.

A few days later, however, they received a phone call from the San Francisco Police.

Their son had died after falling from a building, they were told. The police believed it was a suicide. The grief-stricken parents flew to San Francisco and were taken to the city morgue to identify the body of their son. They recognized him immediately, but to their horror, they discovered something they didn't know—their son had only one arm and one leg.

The parents in this story are like many of us. We find it easy to love those that are good-looking or fun to be around, but we don't like people that inconvenience us or make us feel uncomfortable. We would rather stay away from people who are not as healthy, beautiful, or as smart as we think we are. Thankfully there is someone who won't treat us that way. Someone who love us with an unconditional love that welcomes us into the family forever, regardless of how messed up we are. Tonight, before we go to sleep, pray that God will help give us the strength we need to accept those people that are difficult to love, people like ourselves. Then give thanks that God loves us unconditionally as we turn to him daily for help and support.

Transitioning from teaching and coaching to working part-time at M Den and at U of M in a part-time position has been a new challenge. Being a novice at technology has also caused me to be humble as an employee, since a second grader probably has as much technological experience as I do. As a matter of fact, I used to ask them at school for assistance with computer-related work. When I was coaching, I felt very comfortable with adjustments we made on the field, and I felt comfortable helping student athletes off the field as well. Learning is a lifelong endeavor, so I hope to continue to strive to learn and be patient while I am in the process of doing so.

I know some who will read this book and say, why is it so full of religious matter? I know that I am content with expressing my faith in God and how he has seen me throughout the challenges of life. Some would say your truth is your truth; my truth is my truth.

However, even an atheist, if they are honest with you, would admit that without God, there is no ultimate authority or standard, except each individual's will or view; situational ethics is how I would classify it.

Corrie Ten Boom used to tell the story of the telephone operator who received a daily phone call from a man inquiring about the time. This call came every day about noon. Her curiosity aroused, she asked the man why he called daily at noon, needing the time. He explained, "I am responsible to blow the factory whistle at noon, and I am just ensuring that I am on time each day."

The operator gasped and said, "But I set my watch by your whistle each day."

As this illustration shows, without a clear objective standard, one could get quite a ways off from a standard before their error became evident. Of course, those who teach that every person is a law unto themselves believe that there are limitations to that concept, but it is always "their" limitations. Who is to say that their limitations should have priority over someone else's boundaries or limitations?

The Man and the Birds
by Paul Harvey

The man to whom I'm going to introduce you was not a scrooge, he was a kind and decent, mostly good man. Generous to his family, upright in his dealings with other people. But he did not believe all that incarnation stuff, God became man which the churches proclaim at Christmas Time. Why would God want to become a mere man and live on this wretched earth. It just didn't make sense to him and he was too honest to pretend otherwise. He just could not swallow the Jesus Story, of a Mighty God becoming a little baby in a manger, when he came to this earth to save mankind.

"I'm truly sorry to distress you," he told his wife and kids, "but I am not going to go to church with you this Christmas Eve." He said he would feel like a hypocrite. That he would much rather just stay at home, but he would wait up for them to come back home.

So he stayed and they went to the midnight service without him.

Shortly after the family drove away in the car, snow began to fall. He went to the window to watch the flurries getting heavier and heavier and then he went back to his fireside chair and began to read his newspaper. Minutes later he was startled by a thudding sound… Then another and then another. Sort of like a thump or a thud. At first he thought someone must be throwing snowballs against his living room window. But when he went to the front door to investigate he found a flock of birds huddled miserably in the snow. They had been caught in the storm and in a desperate search for shelter, had tried to fly through his large landscape window.

Well, he could not let the poor creatures lie there and freeze to death, so he remembered the barn where his children stabled their pony. That would provide a warm shelter, if he could direct the birds into it. Quickly he put on a heavy winter coast, boots, and trampled through the deepening snow to the barn. He opened the doors wide and turned on a light, but the birds did not come in to the barn. He figured food would entice them in. So he hurried back to the house, fetched bread crumbs, sprinkled them on the snow, making a trail to the brightly lit door wide open barn of safety. But to his dismay the birds ignored the bread crumbs, and continued to flap around helplessly in the cold snow. He tried catching them, he tried shooing them into the barn by walking around them and waving his arms in that direction. Instead they scattered in different directions, every where but into the safe warm barn.

Then it occurred to him that they were afraid of him. To them he reasoned, I am a stranger and terrifying creature.

If only I could think of some way to let them know that they can Trust me. That I am not trying to hurt them but to help them. But how? Because every move he made tended to frighten them, confuse them more. They just would not follow him no matter what he was doing because they feared him. "If only I could be a bird," he thought to himself; and mingle with them and speak their language. Then, I could tell them not to be afraid of me. Then I could show them the way to the safe, warm barn and save them. But I would have to be one of them, so they could see, and hear and understand me. At that moment the church bells began to ring in the distance. The sound reached his ears above the sound of the blowing winds. He stood there listening to the bells pealing the glad tidings of Christmas Joy. He sank to his knees in the snow. So that is why God came to this earth!

GODLY MENTORS

I was blessed to be a successful football coach and to have been taught by wonderful experienced coaches. I've shared with you earlier the names of coaching mentors. People like Lloyd Carr taught me secondary play, Bill McCartney taught me defensive concepts and inside linebacker play, Milan Vooletich taught me outside linebacker play, Billy Harris taught me secondary play, Ron Vanderlinden taught me inside linebacker play, Jim Hermann taught me some even-front defenses, and Coach Chuck Lori taught me all the basics of force unit play. He taught me the gap responsibilities, alignments, visual and pressure keys for the defensive line, and all the sound fundamentals of reading the offensive line blocking schemes and how to stop those schemes with proper technique; not with blitzes, which seems to be the trend in high school today.

All of these men have something in common, with the exception of Chuck Lori, who I coached with at Pioneer and Huron; all the rest were at the University of Michigan, at one time or another, as Wolverines. Three were head coaches: Lloyd Carr at U of M (winning a national championship in 1997), Bill McCartney at the University of Colorado (winning a national championship in 1990), and Ron Vanderlinden at the University of Maryland. Chuck Lori won state championships in two states, two in Michigan (1984 and 1987) and one in Indiana (1979), at Blackford High School.

The two-state Class A championships in Michigan, Chuck and I worked together, Chuck orchestrating the offense, while I coordinated the defense. The year 1984 was a blowout of Dearborn Fordson with a 38–12 Pioneer victory (then the largest margin of victory in the Class A finals), 1987 was the year I will always remember because we shut out Detroit Catholic Central two times that year, 7–2 in week 3, and 3–0 in the championship game. CC had four Division I players, while we had none that year; although Aaron Bailey, a junior that season, played at the University of Louisville for two years after attending a junior college. He then played in the NFL for the Indianapolis Colts. Shutting out a well-coached Tom Mach team twice was not easy; he has won more Class A or Division I state titles than any other coach.

PREPARATION

I would like to discuss defending a well-coached team we prepared for in 2012 in the first round of the playoffs. We played Monroe High School and defeated them 34–0. Monroe is a Wing-T team coached well by Eric Redman.

First, I will explain our practice format to demonstrate our priorities. We two-platoon, meaning our players start on offense or defense, not both ways. This keeps them fresher, allows them to learn their positions much more thoroughly, and to receive many more repetitions in practice than going both ways allows. In a typical practice session, we would practice from 4:00 p.m. to 7:00 p.m. We had a mandatory study table seventh hour that all players attended five days a week, unless they had a seventh-hour class, which was less than 10 percent of the players. We took a lap at 4:00 p.m. exactly, followed by a brief five-minute stretch and plyometric session. Following, we ran right to our specialty positions for fifteen minutes.

During specialty, the kicking game takes priority over all else. However, everyone has a specialty. Examples: All offensive linemen and defensive force unit players went one-on-one with the basic interior runs, focusing on how to block the front properly, and how to defend that play properly. Emphasis was on trap, inside veer, power, iso, counter, sweep (although with sweep the key, defensively, was staying inside out in pursuit), and zone and zone read. While the ILBs, for example, did the following: align properly in a good low stance, take their read step, attack their gap responsibilities, read their guard keys, fill off the butt of the first down lineman on trap, yell out *pull* when their guard pulled outside and yelled trap when their guard pulled across the ball or center. Step and stack for the QB on inside veer, because they visually saw a closed window in front of them when the DT hit and closed with the OT who was trying to get to him.

Staying square on the QB and *never* overrunning the QB. (Cardinal rule for an ILB is *never* overrun the ball, stay inside out.) Stepping and stacking on power/counter when the OLB wrong arms the kick-out block of the FB or the guard. If his *guard* blocks down, and there is an open window (no one in B gap), he attacks the line and meets the FB in their backfield, trying to isolate on him, the ILB. Work inside out on sweep or jet/fly sweep, staying on their back hip until they turn up.

Step and stack away from an inside zone-blocking play. They take their first two steps with their guards toward their initial gaps and then step and stack away, play side ILB would run to A away (if a force ILB) or same side A (if a scrape ILB), the back side ILB would stack outside of the tackle for the QB keep or RB cutback.

Occasionally if their guard pass sets, they would check draw, then work hook to curl or wall off 3–2, the scrape ILB has to keep his eyes on the QB if the QB scrambles outside his way he is contain man. We call this a "muddle drop" because he works to his hook zone but must attack the QB's inside number if he runs outside the veer defensive tackle. Some coaches do not like this concept of not having a contain DT to one side, but it works well. I learned this from former AA Pioneer defensive player Steve Powers, who coaches in Houston, Texas, high schools where they have twenty spring practices and are on the cutting edge of techniques to stop the spread sets and zone read teams. Steve calls occasionally, and we talk football techniques. I also traveled to Houston, Texas, in 2011 during their spring practice to watch and learn these techniques.

Our defensive linemen would also work on their alignment, first step, gap responsibilities, and their visual and pressure keys. For example, on trap, if they are the play side tackle and their visual key, the OT rips inside to try to get on the ILB, they don't allow it by hitting the OT and following him down inside, closing right off his butt with his eyes inside for either the dive back on veer or the guard pulling to trap him out. He will put his hat across the RB's body on veer, and if trap takes his outside arm and *wrong arms* the trapper, rip it across the trapper's face to force the RB outside where his ILB has stepped and stacked to a closed window. If the DT does not hit the OT, the following happens: the OT kills his ILB, the pulling guard kicks him out, and the RB is screaming upfield to the next level. If double- teamed, the DT or noseguard would grab grass and create a pile, grabbing ankles and not allowing the OL to bounce to the ILBs; if they get too high or don't fight pressure, they will get driven back into the ILBs and lose the LOS, allowing the offense to get movement backward.

OLBs are basically doing the same thing on power and counter that a DT does on trap—hit the TE and close inside with eyes, then to near back, then guard. Our progression key for our OLBs most of the time is TE number 2, near back, guard. They would take a dive back on outside veer (something you don't see much anymore [Temperance Bedford ran it against us in 2012 to keep us honest with our OLBs; they are a well-coached team by Jeff Wood]) or *wrong arm* a trapping guard or a kick-out FB. Chuck Lori ran a lot of outside veer in the '80s, but we were a predominantly two-TE team. I really enjoyed preparing for Bedford because they ran option, and you and to prepare for all the phases of the option, The dive QB and the pitchman. Of course you still had to defend pass and perimeter runs like rocket sweep. The favorite play for Bedford is midline option, where the QB reads ideally the 3T/ DT. If he closes for the FB, the QB keeps it, and in the Georgia Tech style, flexbone style option offense, they insert one or two slots on the ILB and the fold defender. The key to playing the option well is have at least one and a half players on each phase of the option, in case someone misses their assignment, and change the QB's read occasionally so that the dive key now takes the QB, for example.

OLBs are now almost like strong safeties these days in their athleticism, because you need that much speed on the field with all the spread formation personnel. For example, they might have four or five wide receivers on offense.

While all of this is going on, the kicking game is a top priority. Kickoffs and kick returners, punters, long snappers and punt returners, X PT and FG with short snappers and holders, QBs and wide receivers, DBs covering the WRs and DBs working on their DB coverage skills.

At 4:25, there was a quick water break of 2 minutes, followed by a 20–30 minute individual technique session. At approx. 4:50 p.m. group sessions were run for 10 minutes: turnover drills, tackling, hit & shed drill, ball security, stalk blocks & stalk & go, screen passes and defending screens, highest point ball drills, strip & recover, fetal, scoop & score, cup drill tackling, goal line techniques for defensive line (root hog, low).

Offense and defense were specified in the drills: 5 p.m. 1st and 2nd offense vs 1st & 2nd defense skeletal pass (7on7); 5:15 Team Offense vs. Scout defense, Team Defense vs. Scout offense 6:25 Tuesday=Team Punt, Wednesday=Punt Return 6:50 Defensive Pursuit vs. Scout O & 1st. O 7:00 All Up Monday, all kicking game was reviewed, along with weight training, film, and a walk through of upcoming opponent.

Thursday: all kicking game was reviewed, along with team O and D. Winning edge= Game Situations, two min. O versus D; keys to victory; coaches talk in locker room; team meal in the cafeteria; awards from last week presented; tutoring available to all student athletes

Saturday: 9:00 a.m.–10:00 a.m., weight training and running offense; film review defense, 10:00 a.m.–11:00 a.m.; switch, 11:00 a.m.–11:15 a.m.; team meeting 11:20 a.m.–12:00 FCA.

Optional meeting Sunday: 7:00 p.m.–11:00 p.m., coaches' meeting, film review, awards are completed and posted in the locker room, as well as team stats.

This format has helped us win a few games over the years as well as two state titles and five undefeated seasons and one unscored- upon season.

Successful seasons are fun, and the players and coaches get excited by the success, as does the community.

What is true and lasting success?

Successful People

In 1923, a very important meeting was held at the Edgewater Beach Hotel in Chicago. Attending this meeting were nine of the world's most successful financiers.

Those present were the President of the largest independent Steel company; The president of the largest utility company, the president of the largest gas company, the greatest wheat speculator, the president of the New York Stock Exchange, president of the bank of international settlements, and a member of the Certainly, we must admit that here were gathered a group of the world's most successful men; at least, men who had found the secret of making money.

Let us see what happened to these men 25 years later. The president of the largest independent steel company, Charles Schwab died in bankruptcy and lived on borrowed money for five years before his death. The president of the greatest utility company, Samuel Insull, died a fugitive from justice, penniless in a foreign land. The president of the largest gas company, Howard Hobson, went insane, the greatest wheat speculator, Arthur Cotton, died abroad insolvent. The president of the New York Stock Exchange, Richard Whitney, was released from Sing-Sing Penitentiary.

The member of the presidents cabinet, Albert Fall, was pardoned so that he could die at home. The greatest "Bear" on Wall Street, Jesse Livermore died a suicide, the president of the Bank of International Settlements, Leon Fraser, e head of the greatest monopoly, Ivan Kruger, died a suicide. All of them learned well the "art of making a living," but none of them learned "how to live!"

Success as defined by a Semitic king over 2,500 years ago: successful and happy are those who reject the advice of evil men, who do not follow their example or join those who have no use for God. Instead they find joy in obeying the Word of God, and they study it day and night, they are like trees planted beside a stream, they bear fruit in due season, their leaves never dry up. They succeed in everything they do!

This is quite a contrast to our Chicago businessmen and their fate. No one gets out alive. That is a sobering thought for all of us to consider. What then is important, you might ask yourself? Does it matter how I conduct myself on a daily basis? Does it matter how I treat others? Does it matter what my character is like? We thirst for answers to these questions. We all want to experience more than just the fleeting excitement of that which this world has to offer. Drugs, sex, power, prestige, material possessions, and wealth are all temporary. They bring some sense of satisfaction, but nothing that lasts. "Can't get no satisfaction," the Rolling Stones bellowed out decades ago; a good song but also a reminder, much to their consternation, that which is satisfying is usually the peace that is offered only in the spiritual domain. Sheep thirst and become restless and set out in search of water to satisfy their thirst. If there is not a shepherd around to guide them to the right spot, the clean pure water that satisfies and is healthy, they will often end up drinking from polluted areas where they can pick up diseases and parasites that disturb their inner digestive tracks and destroy their peace; they become agitated.

Also in this manner, our Good Shepherd let us know that we, too, search for life-giving water that does satisfy.

Happy are they that hunger and thirst after righteousness, for they shall be satisfied. (Matthew 5:6)

Jesus Christ himself said, "If any man thirst, let him/her come to me and drink." Spiritually he was reminding us that drinking means to accept or believe what he has taught. Most of us that are thirsty are unsure of where to look or what they are looking for. We, too, like the sheep, will drink from any dirty pool of water to satisfy our desires. Saint Augustine of Africa reminds us "that God has made us for himself, and our souls (mind, will and emotions) are restless until they rest in Thee/God." In the Psalms, David tells us that the Good Shepherd will lead us beside still, quiet, life-giving waters; only he knows where to lead us, if we are willing to follow.

In this world, it is often those who find time to feed on his Word that are experiencing the most joy and are serene in their ability to cope with life's challenges. Just as a flock of sheep are content when they are in a safe, quiet, refreshing sight; so, too, are we content when we surrender our wills to ruminate on God's Word in a peaceful setting, whether it is early in the morning or late in the evening. But the irony of life is that most us try to satisfy our thirst by pursuing every other sort of desire that this world has to offer, sometimes knowing that it really won't satisfy. Sports, for example, are an obsession for many people, when they go to stadiums and scream and shout their support for their team. When they win, they are temporarily satisfied, and when they lose, they are agitated. These experiences of excitement are hollow, empty, and temporary at best.

When we won our state championship at AA Pioneer in 1984 and 1987, my wife reminded me that I was content for about a week, and then I began to think about next year. Now that is how you stay on top by never being satisfied with your success, but it also puts one on a never-ending roller coaster of success that never truly satisfies.

The great record producer from Motown Lamont Dozier had many, many number 1 hits and is in the Rock & Roll Hall of Fame, said that he was on the roller coaster of success and could not get off. Instead of his success bringing satisfaction, he was always trying to raise the standard higher and never was satisfied. The ancient prophet Jeremiah put it succinctly, "My people have forsaken my life-giving waters, and hewed out broken cisterns that can hold no water." In today's society, this is the picture we see—people trying to find satisfaction in this world's endeavors and being resistant to Truth as Jesus Christ would present it. "What is truth?" the Roman prefect Pontius Pilate asked in the first century after the death of Jesus Christ. "I am the Truth," is what

Jesus told us. Do we choose to believe him? I am, the name of God, is what he referred to himself as, the Alpha and Omega.

The same people that scream and shout for their football team on Saturday or Sunday and worship at the temple of sports but consider someone who worships God as being simple or extreme. It is okay to scream and shout for athletes but not for our Creator. It is okay to spend hours watching TV and movies but not okay to spend time in prayer or listening to God's direction. He is pleased when we choose to walk in union with his will and attempt to live holy lives set apart from the ways of this world. I will dwell in the house of the Lord forever; that is my goal, and I will attempt to attain it with his help and mercy!

Now you might ask, what makes us so special that of all the creatures in the world, we are the only ones who are able to communicate with our Creator. We are the only ones that have a two-way relationship with him. The rocks can't do that. The rivers can't do that. A monkey can't do that. We are the only ones who can consciously say we are creatures, we have a Creator. Yet amazing as it is, we usually do not call God our Creator, but rather in Christendom, we call him Father. How in the world can we speak to an almighty being with such familiarity? He is the maker of the sun, and the moon and the stars, the galaxies, this entire universe as we know it. It seems ridiculous to refer to him as Father and us as his sons and daughters. The solution to this paradox is Christmas. Here God took on the form of a human being in the person of Jesus Christ.

We are all God's children, but as Christians, we get to share in this special relationship with the Father in a uniquely special way, if we choose to. Since Jesus is the Son of God, although he took on our human nature, he also imparted on us his divine nature.

He blessed us with the Holy Spirit to bring us into this family of God's. Why is this important? Because it changes our identity to citizens of our Lord and King in heaven, Jesus Christ. If we became heirs to a billionaire here on earth, someone like Warren Buffet, Bill Gates, or some king, we would have limitless resources available to us.

Well, spiritually we do have access to a King in heaven and his kingdom for eternity. Do all Christians live that way? Obviously not, but they have the right to. All of us were created to be citizens of heaven, but many of us choose not to be. Every person was created to be a king or queen in heaven, but many will choose to follow the enemy—the devil—into hell and be wretched souls there. Many powerful invisible forces are working against us. These forces will stop at nothing to achieve their objective, to prevent souls from sharing in this eternal union with God. As C. S. Lewis said, "Every person is destined to be a King or Queen in heaven or a wretched slave in hell." As sure as you are reading these words right now, there is an invisible battle raging all around you, a battle between heaven and hell, angels and demons, darkness and light, evil and God's grace. A battle where there has never been nor never will be a truce, a battle that goes on in every town, city, state, country in the world—an invisible battle for your soul! As we talked about in the "Man and the Birds" story, God found a way to communicate his love for us by sending his Son to die for our sins. He loves us that much.

Satan is very smart. For example, during Christmastime, he and his demons prowl around the world seeking souls to destroy. Because so many people are happy at this time, he tries to get them to do good things for others, lots and lots of good things, so many that they forget what the season and the gift-giving is really all about. Although this giving is kind and can help to bring families closer together, people are so busy doing so many special things that there is no time for them to be prayerful and think of God's holiness. He loves to distort our priorities in this fashion; he loves to take something good by nature and make us think it is the most taint thing in life. Examples: He tempts some to make food the most important thing in their life. He tempts some to make sex the most important thing. He tempts some to make money the most important, some power, some with work, some with art, some with nature, some with animal rights, some with other worthy causes. These are all good things, but done at the wrong time or in the wrong way or with the wrong person or motive, it can destroy your soul. It really doesn't matter to the devil what is most important to you. The only thing he wants to make sure is that God is not the most important in your life. If God is anything but number 1 in your life, then your priorities are screwed up, and you need an attitude adjustment.

The reason we need to keep God number 1 is to remember that he will forgive us for our sins over and over again, regardless of what the devil says. Satan will try to tell us that God is fed up with forgiving us; he has lost his patience with us. I have found that when I am trying to live a holy life, and the times when I have had the most success dealing with temptation, that I felt the most attacks leveled at me from the enemy. He knows our weaknesses and when we are feeling pretty spiritual in our endeavors, that he rallies the troops to discourage us. We have to remember that God will always forgive us if we ask him to.

Consider the difference between Peter and Judas, for example. Judas betrayed Christ with a kiss and that led to his arrest, crucifixion, and death on the cross. Peter denied ever even knowing Jesus after he had said he would never deny Christ. Both were guilty of sin, but one, Judas gave up; he became despondent. Peter repented of his denial and asked forgiveness. Judas may have been forgiven, we do not really know; his actions demonstrated despair. Peter went on to lead the early church, and Judas killed himself. We have to always turn to God for forgiveness and mercy, and he is always faithful to forgive. Our lives are the result of the choices we make. To blame and accuse others, the environment, or other extrinsic factors is to choose to empower those things to control us.

Closing thought: God loved us so much *he* sent his only begotten Son to die for us so that whoever believes in *him* will not perish but will have *everlasting* life, for God did not send *his* Son to condemn us but to save us. *Praise God!*
2016

I would like to begin to discuss current issues as well as that which has taken place in this past year. My wife Pam and I, have begun to consider a possible move to the Raleigh, North Carolina, area. Our eldest daughter lives there with her family, and we certainly miss them all. In Raleigh, we have two grandchildren, Vivian, six, and Greyson, three. Her husband, Michael Dascola has a great job with BB & T Bank and has moved up the ladder there quickly. His father, Bob, and grandfather Dominic Dascola have run Dascola Barbers in Ann Arbor for years. We miss the grandkids and only see them once or twice a year at best.

I have spoken with two football coaches in the area and have the possibility of coaching at one of the schools. Both head coaches are looking for a defensive coordinator to help bring their programs to another level of excellence. Sanderson High School is a public school in Raleigh, while Cardinal Gibbons is a Catholic high school in the Raleigh area. Both schools have young men that are in need of guidance and training both on and off the field. Sanderson High School is a diverse but talented group of young men, while Gibbons is a private school with a hefty price tag for tuition of over $20,000 per year. Although their needs may vary, both schools have student athletes needing direction and encouragement. Two of my former assistants at Ann Arbor Pioneer High School are also interested in moving to the Raleigh, North Carolina, area. Jerrard Harrison and Vince Wortmann are both considering the move South. The warmer weather is certainly an attraction, and the Raleigh, Durham, Chapel Hill research triangle is a great place to live and raise a family. Jerrard and Vince were my codefensive coordinators at Ann Arbor Pioneer. They both work hard and are extremely loyal assistant coaches.

Jerrard played inside linebacker at Ann Arbor Huron during the 2001, 2002 seasons. He was defensive captain and called the signals in the huddle. Vince started in the defensive secondary at Ann Arbor Pioneer during the 1985, 1986 seasons. He also played some wide receiver his senior season. He then received a full athletic football scholarship to the University of Cincinnati to become a Bearcat. Vince has a job as a videographer at military boot camps throughout the summer months. He did a great job with all our video equipment HUDL at Pioneer.

I am not technologically inclined at all. I still have a flip phone as a cell phone. In today's society, where there is little trust and appreciation of different cultures and races, it is inspiring to know that two young black men want to travel to Raleigh to continue our system of coaching young men. I feel that unless we can grow in our trust and appreciation for one another, our society will stagnate. I pray this does not happen.

This evening, after Mass at Saint Andrew's Church in Saline, Michigan, I spoke with former PE coordinator at Ann Arbor Pioneer High School, Mrs. Bonnie Pendleton. We have talked before about faith and family but spent quite a bit of time tonight discussing race. Most whites and many blacks are uncomfortable talking about racial issues. Bonnie was born and raised in Baton Rouge, Louisiana. She shared with me many experiences growing up there. She first talked to me about her father, who is growing older and in need of care due to eyesight and other aging problems.

Care for the aged is one issue that should also be given a lot more priority. Our parents spend years caring and nurturing us as we grow up, only too often to find us too busy to care for them when they are in need of our care. My mother lived to be ninety-six, as I stated earlier, but had great care from my brothers Sam and Dennis especially, and my sister Janine and I were also frequent visitors. Bonnie was saying that her father was Creole (a white descendant of French settlers in Louisiana). He could pass for white or black, and this provided him with many positive experiences, while the typical black person in that area was afforded negligible consideration. She told me how in high school, the graduation ceremonies and school dances were all white or all black, and many people did not want integrated schools in the first place.

Bonnie said something that I had not realized myself, that one reason parents wanted separate schools was to prevent their white child from discerning for themselves the character and behavior of the black student that was sitting right next to them all day in class. Once they discovered for themselves that there were wonderful black students and wonderful white students, as well as problematic black students and problematic white students, it was not a skin problem; it was, in fact, a "sin problem" that existed. Bonnie and her husband, Carl, have just retired and are planning on moving to Louisiana at least part of the year. I had the pleasure of coaching their son, Justin, in football at Pioneer; he attended college in Alabama and is a bright student in prelaw. Bonnie and I actually taught PE in A2, at Bryant Elementary School, the same year, 1986. She taught PE in the afternoon there, while I taught in the morning at Bryant, before traveling to Pioneer to teach speech in the afternoon. I watched her and was impressed because she did not put up with any nonsense during class; she was strict, and so was I when I taught there, but we were also caring and consistent with all the students. I know the willingness to travel to a student's home at night and meet with parents and/or grandparents to let the kids know I was serious, and cared. Since football is what I spent a great deal of my time teaching, I want to connect this issue with coaching. Coaching football is not just about teaching Xs and Os; it is about teaching character and life skills of hard work and relationships. With relationships in mind, I'll turn to my experience with Vince and Jerrard.

Team unity is a key concept in having a great program. Players must believe in their coaches and trust them to have their best interests at heart. Players cannot pretend to care about one another on the football field while having nothing to do with one another off the field, as in the locker room or classroom. In 1980, at Pioneer, I watched how players isolated black and white in the locker room, classroom, weight room, and on the buses. I called the kids out about it, saying you cannot be a team on the field and apart off the field. It took some doing, but change occurred.

One thing that we established in the '80s at Ann Arbor Pioneer was this unified concept. I believe the healthy respect that Vincent, Jerrard, and I, have for one another will be manifested in the program while we work together. It certainly was manifested in Ann Arbor Pioneer in 2011 and 2012. Jerrard has a good job with AT&T, while Vincent will be able to do some teaching and instruction at the high school. I also would love to do some part-time teaching at either school.

As I said, back at Ann Arbor Pioneer in 1980, there was no unity, and there was no discussion about it; players segregated in the locker rooms to their own little groups of black and white. We addressed the lack of unity the first season, and by 1981, there was a marked difference on and off the field. Sean McCabe(white) and Robbie Davis(black) in the mid-'80s, both excellent football players, went to the middle schools to address some racial taunting that was taking place. The younger kids saw the two of the older boys befriend the student that was picked on, and it ended shortly thereafter. We, as older, more mature, and hopefully wiser men and women, need to manifest the appropriate conduct for those that are younger to follow. In a high school football program, the seniors need to exemplify the standard of behavior that the coaching staff wants to have permeate the team. Each season, each team will have a different disposition and a different persona, and the seniors, along with the coaches, will determine just how effective they will be. However, it all begins with the head coach; if he allows disrespect, disunity, profanity, selfishness, lack of attention to detail, determination, and character, the team will never be as successful as is possible. The head coach must establish a healthy connection with the upperclassmen.

Simply put, "kids don't care how much you know, until they know how much you care!" The days of the negative motivator that uses put-downs and critical verbal tirades of profanity is about as useful as mammary glands on a bull. Even if they win games, the coach has not developed any lasting character or citizenry for the future.

There is very little that is more satisfying than seeing former student athletes that are now good husbands and fathers and producing well in our society. They use the same determination, hard work, unselfishness, and godly character to reinforce and enhance the depth of their families' efficacious future.

A.M.U. Florida (I was Michigan's head football scout for Tom Monaghan)

While working at the M Den at Briarwood, I have the pleasure of working with Rick and Bob Stites' daughters. Both are intelligent, hardworking, enjoyable young ladies to work with. Mrs. Wendy Roberts is our manager, and she is a former Pioneer student from the late '80s. She is a joy to work for; she has established a very efficient and cooperative workforce at Briarwood and keeps things moving quickly and efficiently. Her friendly demeanor is coupled with a creative and energetic setting for staff and customers. I enjoy greeting and meeting people throughout the evening hours. What has been exciting for me is to have many former students and athletes, as well as parents, from the local Ann Arbor and surrounding area stop in when they are shopping. I believe I have been able to encourage sales with many of these people as well. It is quite challenging at times when a student from twenty-plus years ago stops in and says hello, because often I have not seen them since they were eleven to twelve years of age, while now they are in their twenties, thirties, or forties. Many former students and athletes offer encouragement, hugs, and often prayers. I am so grateful to be in that environment. There are lots of high school and college students working at M Den. It is fun to observe their dynamics in day-to-day interaction. I hope that I have been a good influence with the kids. Some days, I have more energy than others, but I want to try and serve by my actions and words of encouragement. The arrival of Jim Harbaugh as the new U of M football head coach has been an inducement for the football program and for sales at M Den. If he wears the hat, sweatshirt, or other type of shirt, then people wanted to wear it too. They are inspired by his intensity and enthusiasm. The 2016 season provided a schedule that should allow U of M to start fast and grow. They opened with Hawaii at home and followed that with several games against weaker opponents. Big rivals like MSU didn't come around until week 9, after Illinois and a bye week.

I am looking forward to traveling to Raleigh and meeting with the head coach from Sanderson High School, Coach Ben Kohlstadt. He is from Wisconsin. Former Ann Arbor Pioneer football player Steve Powers coached with Ben as a defensive coordinator and did a great job of coaching. They made the playoffs for the first time in years and, during the season, defeated the eventual state runner-up in Class 4A (similar to Division I here in Michigan) in a close game. The team ran the Wing T, and Steve used our defensive game plan that was so effective against Monroe High School in 2011 and 2012. I miss working with the high school kids and preparing them for competition each week on the field, as well as preparing them for the daily challenges in the classroom, off the field, at home with family, and in their respective neighborhoods.

As a teacher, I felt it was important to reach all students, especially those struggling behaviorally. Having been asked to speak at the U of M PE workshop in 2010 and 2011, by Ms. Pat Van Volkinburg, the head of student-teacher placement, I prepared for "Dealing with Difficult Students." This topic was exciting to discuss with fellow colleagues at the workshop. Ms. Van, as we called her, had sent me a student teacher every semester for many years, and I enjoyed that responsibility and dynamic interaction with these young students. They were highly motivated and did an excellent job of developing classroom management skills. Classroom management is so important to establish a positive learning environment for all the students. Being proactive and finding something positive to say to difficult students is paramount. These students are going to get your attention one way or another, so better to initiate praise than constant scolding. When they come in the room, meet them and give them a high five, compliment something they are wearing, or be alert to any positive dynamic you notice. Now when they misbehave, they will be much more amenable to your correction and guidance than if you never have anything positive to say. You are showing them they are important to you. Visit them at home, sit with them in the lunchroom or on the playground. Listen to what they have to say, then they, too, will listen to what you have to say.

Thurston P.E. Teacher Paul

Thurston P.E. class

In 2007, Mrs. Pat Manley and I sat in her office at Thurston Elementary to discuss ways that we could address activities that, while benefiting everyone, would have a positive effect on the African American community and their children. We discussed the importance of dance and decided to implement a ten-week unit on Club Ballroom Dance with "Mr. and Mrs. Smooth" (a.k.a. Calvin and Jackie Siebert from the Inkster area). We had one day a week, from April to May, where the fifth graders were taught Club Ballroom Dance, as well as such individual steps as the cha-cha slide, the cupid shuffle, the turbo shuffle, and others. At the end of ten weeks, we had a dinner dance in the evening with the parents and their children. Children dressed up for the occasion, with girls wearing dresses and boys wearing a dress shirt and slacks; some wore jackets and ties as well. The gentlemen were taught how to ask for a dance, and the ladies were taught how to respond politely to their request. The first year, we had soul food from an establishment in Ypsilanti; they provided greens, chicken, ribs, mac and cheese, and some pizza.

All the families had a ball dancing, eating, and watching their children enjoy themselves immensely. The parents were taught the line dances at the beginning of the evening, providing some exercise for themselves. After the first year of doing this, the kids looked forward to that special night, and I know that it was remembered for a long time because many have brought it up to me at the M Den. What a great way to stay fit, dancing.

The Turkey Trot was also a special event that my predecessor began, Mr. Mike Bledow. He was the former PE teacher at Thurston Elementary. The Turkey Tro" took place the week before Thanksgiving and was a great opportunity to teach kids fitness and healthy eating, as well as caring for the less fortunate in the community. We changed a few things such as awards to all who started and finished the race regardless of where they finished. We also had snacks and decided to change from donuts and pop to apples, fruit, juice (apple). We had many families donate turkeys to the needy and poor in the community. All of these families were eligible for a raffle of ten awards from local merchants in the neighborhood. The kids walk/ran a mile around the neighborhood, while parent cheerleaders cheered them on and kept a close eye on the kids as they ran/walked. Children could go as fast or slow as they wanted, but all finished and were treated with refreshments of healthy food.

Back in high school, I was fortunate enough to have some wonderful teachers that helped me academically, spiritually, and athletically. Sister

Cecelia was always in my corner helping me to mature and become more focused. After messing around in a science class called IPS in ninth grade, she made sure that I could retake the class my senior year and make amends academically.

She allowed my friend Paul Nanasi, who attended the University of Minnesota on a football scholarship, and myself to make up the class, and we both buckled down and did well our senior year. Paul was a super athlete, with a 6'2", 225-plus frame, and speed to burn; he could run like a running back. After a rough night the previous evening, Paul would show up at morning workouts at 7:00 a.m. and go through a strenuous session without blinking an eye, despite indulging in beverages and other supplements, little to no sleep, and would do his fifteen-minute run after conditioning in his bare feet on the track, ouch! Thank God for teachers like Sister Cecelia that put up with us.

After watching the ESPN show 30 for 30, "The Gospel According to Mac," I was mesmerized by how effective Coach Mac was in developing great relationships with his players in Colorado. He became head coach in Boulder, Colorado, in the early '80s. He turned around a mediocre program in a few years and eventually won a national championship in 1990. His faith in the Lord allowed him to reach even the most challenging young men in his program. Coach Mac ran a tight ship at CU, but his players appreciated his discipline and expertise.

In the 30 for 30 program, most of the athletes that were interviewed were black. Mac had a strong calling in creating Promise Keepers, to help men become better husbands and fathers. He also had a strong inspiration to have Christians grow across denominational lines and to cross racial barriers. As a coach, he hired many excellent black assistants and brought a plethora of great black athletes to Boulder, which were largely responsible for their success in the 1990 national championship. After Coach Mac was done with the Promise Keeper movement, he traveled around the country and visited intercity black churches and taught about racial reconciliation. Building the black community and its families through the church has been the history of our African American brothers for decades.

As Dr. Alan Keyes states in his book *Masters of the Dream: The Strength and Betrayal of Black America:*

> Despite poverty, woefully inadequate funds and an environment decidedly hostile to black education, we know that black Americans consistently made progress against illiteracy in generations following emancipation. Character formation and moral discipline were the keys that sustained black commitment to self-improvement. Today with "value free" education and teaching sex ed while eliminating their moral dimension. Young people acquire information without character formation. They are encouraged to be preoccupied with their passions and desires but without any sense of the moral faculty that can discipline and guide the passions. They learn self-awareness but without self-control. Character building was at the core of the black educational tradition. In the black community, for instance, no important enterprise is begun without prayer. Schools belong to the community not to the bureaucrats, if the community and parents in the community with the Churches guidance promoted education, character would be reasserted.
>
> The God fearing, family valuing, hardworking black majority has thus been the "invisible man" in the typical image of America.

Of course this will embolden many and the press to cry separation of church and state, even though it is not in the constitution.

When I coached at Pioneer and Huron, we always had a pregame prayer led by a student athlete, and the kids always wanted this to be a part of their football experience. Despite our diversity religiously and culturally, we had a healthy respect for our differences, and there was great moral development. How one talks, dresses, and acts are synonymous with character development. We never allowed shorts or pants to be worn below the butt (as is common in many youths today); we did not cuss and swear at student athletes and did not allow any profanity from them. Also unselfishness is taught on and off the football field. A player's skin color has nothing to do with displaying character. Again I quote Dr. Martin Luther King Jr., "I dream of the day when my children are not judged by the color of their skin—but by the content of their character!"

Coach Mac made great strides in communicating this to his players at Colorado and while at U of M as defensive coordinator under Bo Schembechler. As Coach Bobby Bowden said, "Don't let football become your God because if you do, you'll also likely become miserable." Coach Mac always would begin a conversation with me by quoting a Scripture passage. I listened and eventually began to understand that the passage of Scripture was often exactly what I needed to hear.

> God's Word is alive, active, shaper than any two-edged sword, able to penetrate even to dividing soul and spirit, joints and marrow; it judges the thoughts and attitudes of the heart.

My thoughts and attitudes were being examined daily as I began to read his Word and allow it to be my guide. My heart was being examined, and looking back, I am grateful that God provided such a wonderful role model for me to follow. Now I've made many mistakes over the years. Many choices that I would like to change but I cannot. I am so grateful to my Lord for his mercy and grace (unmerited favor). I know I don't deserve it, but I also know God sent his Son to die for my sins when I did not deserve it, not because I had reached some level of perfection but while I was a lowly sinner. Many of us can't forgive others for wrongs they have done to us, but many of us can't forgive ourselves for our own sins, wrongdoing, or transgressions. We beat ourselves up with condemnation and punishment rather than clemency or compassion.

On the cover of his book *Sold Out*, Bill McCartney is described as having it all by this world's standards. He was a successful college football coach, famous, wealthy, and respected in his profession. Yet having it all, he looked in his wife's eyes and saw loneliness, pain, and despair.

Having confronted others with the emptiness of a lukewarm life, Mac was forced to face a startling fact—he had become a slave to the system, football. The essence of Sold Out was a guide for men to discipline themselves as believers in God's transforming power, willing to sacrifice all for God's loving intimate relationship. Coach Mac demonstrated this by turning away from the aspirations of college football to commit all to his wife and family, and most importantly his Lord God.

I have looked into my wife's face and seen pain and loneliness as well. Many times, I was so engrossed in coaching and winning high school football games that I did not spend quality time with my wife and kids. Pam was always a stalwart support of my endeavors as a teacher and coach. She sacrificed much for those goals that I had placed in my life. She was a wonderful mother and a supportive wife. I know that we have made strides at appreciating each other. I desire to please her each day and remind myself as Psalm 62:1 states, "My soul finds rest in God alone." I give thanks to God daily for my wife, Pamela Test. Do we have gratitude for all God has done for us?

The story of Jesus healing the ten lepers in Luke 17:11 reminds us that we all need to give thanks and have gratitude for God's healing power.

As Jesus traveled between Samaria and Galilee, he was going into a village, ten menthe had leprosy met him. They stood at a distance and called out a loud voice, Jesus, Master, Son of God have mercy on us! When He saw them He said, "Go show yourselves to the priests" and as they went they were cleansed. One of them when he saw he was healed came back praising God in a loud voice. He threw himself at Jesus' feet and thanked him. He was a Samaritan, (a foreigner). Jesus asked, "were not all ten lepers cleansed? Where are the other nine? Was no one found to return and give praise to God except this foreigner?" Then He said, "Rise and go your faith has made you well."

This passage of scripture reminds us that most often, few give thanks to God for a variety of reasons. Let's examine this more fully with a related story about the ten lepers.

So where were the other nine lepers that had been healed?

One of the lepers, now clean, went off to build a new life for himself, seeking work, a new place to live, and putting down roots for himself. He hoped also for a family. He became so busy building a new life that he forgot the wonderful blessing he had just received.

Another leper was immediately overwhelmed with fear and worry. He said, "What do I do now? I cannot beg anymore. I have to find work, but I have no skills. I have never learned how to do anything since I was young. Who will hire me? How will I eat?" So fearful and worried was the once-unclean leper that he was paralyzed from doing anything productive. So he remained huddled at the gate, afraid and left alone, just like a leper.

Still another leper, realizing that he was now clean, determined to even the score with everyone that had ever laughed at him, scorned him, ignored him, inflicted cruelties and indignities on him over the years because of his illness. "They will pay for what they did to me," he vowed. I will get even with them, if it's the last thing I do." Obsessed with vengeance, he never, for a moment, experienced any joy or appreciation in his cure from leprosy. He wanted everyone to receive payback for their unkindness.

One leper, finally freed from his sufferings, ran as far and as fast away from the place as he could. All he wanted to do was forget his old life of misery and everyone and everything about it. He made himself deaf to the cries of those suffering around him, including lepers. Try as he might, no matter how fast or far he ran, he could still hear their pleas for help, and he ignored them.

Of course, there was one leper who went out and celebrated, celebrated, and celebrated. His newfound joy lasted as long as the wine and other sources of intoxication lasted. Once that all disappeared, so did the camaraderie and fellowship. He now had to face his new life, lost and alone.

There was one leper, who did not believe he was made clean. *Why would anyone, least of all God, want to do this for me? There had to be a catch.* So he did nothing; he just waited and waited for his leprosy to return. In his own mind, he was never healed.

So the nine lepers went their own separate ways but without a sense of gratitude for the miracle they had just experienced. The miracle did not last very long. For their fears, anger, unbelief, their repressions, skepticisms, misplaced hope, and values just made them lepers all over again.

Contrast this to the leper that fell at Jesus's feet with gratitude and joy. He was grateful to God and received his blessing.

As 1 Thessalonians 5:16–18 says, "Be joyful always, pray continually, give thanks in all circumstances for this is God's will for you in Christ Jesus."

I recently read an article that was written in the aftermath of "The Brawl." It was written by John U. Bacon, an Ann Arbor Huron graduate. I know and have respected John over the years as a writer and guest speaker. He, however, commented on the aftermath of the game and really didn't know the facts. He stated that it was a weak answer for me to say that "I did not call those plays" to the Huron head coach.

First of all, I said I did not call that play (singular), because I did not. It was my offensive coordinator that called it, and he called every other play that night, not me. I had an offensive and defensive coordinator on each side of the ball. That I said play is quite significant because right after that play was run (a long pass into the end zone, the officials called defensive interference, and we had a first down in scoring position). I immediately ran down the sideline toward our offense and called for taking a knee or what we called safe. Prior to that, the Huron coach was screaming from his sideline at the previous play that had been called. We took a knee twice, and the clock ran out. That is what I had taken control over after the one play was called.

So John is wrong when he assumes that I was not in charge of my team or that I ran the score up, which I did not do—35–6 is not running up the score. The previous season, it was 56–6, and he did not shake my hand after the game. He was not just pointing a finger; he was cussing with the F-word and pushing me backward at the time my assistant "pushed him away." There was definitely not a punch; the video confirms that completely. He was protecting me by his actions. If someone were cussing John's father out and pushing him around, what would he do? I hope he would protect him, not walk away and watch. My assistant coach has said I am like a father to him.

Also what was said about the captains and athletic directors was inaccurate. First, only the Huron AD spoke and led the discussion about making amends. Second, how can you make amends when there is no asking for forgiveness. When my children grew up and did something wrong, they had to ask for forgiveness from the injured party; this never happened. Also to bring up the Dexter game as an example of running up a score is weak, real weak; one, the score was 54–0 in the middle of the second quarter, everyone played, and only 2 TDs were scored in the last two and a half quarters with a running clock. Also John has no idea what took place at Dexter to a fine man, Tom Barbeiri. He was lied about and treated inappropriately by an assistant coach and an administrator. We did celebrate for his sake, not to display poor sportsmanship.

When you do not know the facts it is best to be quiet! Some forget it was a freshman at QB, late in the game to get some experience before the playoffs started in two weeks, which we were in, and Huron, at 0–9, was not. John, I have always enjoyed your books and speaking, but your comments about the incident were ill informed and inaccurate at best. Maybe as a Huron graduate, you can appreciate that when we were at Huron, we beat Pioneer three years in a row—2000, 2001, 2002—and that has not happened since. I surely wish the whole incident did not happen, but let us at least know the facts, not the spin. Look at what the officials said about the two teams in their report.

There is a lot more to coaching football than winning and losing, but winning is important in our society. Just look at your two books, John, about Coach Rodriguez and Coach Hoke; they are gone. However, my players can attest to what I am about and what I share with them about education, family, life, death, faith, and commitment, as well as dealing with adversity, like this whole ordeal. Yes, I was in charge of my team, but as I have said repeatedly said in Soul Food, we are not in control of every jot and little aspect of what goes on each and every moment of our lives.

Let me repeat that—there was a physical altercation before my assistant pushed the Huron coach away from me. It is evident in the video that we watched after the incident happened. A Huron player was swinging at one of our players in the handshaking line. As my mentor Coach Chuck Lori had said, "The big eye don't lie." My assistant did not get pulled away from the confrontation; he walked away on his own. He did not return to the fray in any way afterward. He only acted in a defensive mode. The *truth will,* eventually, always be discernible.

Soul food is great for the mind, body, spirit, and soul.

Joseph (how adversity was used by God to his purposes)

Sometimes it is difficult to understand God's purposes for challenges and adversity in our life. When life gets hard, we often tend to get angry and wonder how long the difficulty will last. Our God wants us to focus on him in times of trouble; by so doing, we will discover that he is doing important spiritual molding during these most frustrating times of life. The storms in our life can help create in us a deep desire to draw closer to our source of comfort. When circumstances are beyond our control, what we really rely on will surface and become most evident. Our faith will sustain us if it is our true source of joy. "The Joy of the Lord is our strength," the Scripture teaches us.

In the great story of the life of Joseph in the Old Testament, we see a great example of what man intended for bad, God meant for good (Genesis 50:20). There will be times when our world seems upside down and when we do not succeed. Times when God will use the storms to transform us more completely into his image and likeness. Often when everything is going smooth and life is good, we will spend less time in fellowship with our Lord and start to rely only on our self; we become self-satisfied. Let's look at Joseph from an early age.

He was only seventeen when he would come to his father and give a negative report regarding his older brothers. He was a tattletale, and no one likes a tattletale. Two criteria create a tattletale: self-righteousness and self-vindication. Joseph was self-righteous; however, we should be encouraged to know that God can use a self- righteous person for his ends. In Genesis, we are told that Joseph brought a negative report to his father, yet God still uses Joseph to establish his plans for Israel in the future. Joseph was his father's favorite child. He often wasted his time and became spoiled by his father. How much time do we waste every day with behavior that is not pleasing to God? Do we prepare ourselves to be able to witness by our lives that which is important to us?

Preparation is very important in football as well. We only play as well on Friday night as we practice the entire week before the game. The famous basketball coach from UCLA John Wooden was said to have practiced so intensely that his players were relieved by the pace of the game compared to the vigorous spirited workouts and simulation of the upcoming game. Preparation leads to peace of mind as a player and as a coach. When you prepare with the focus necessary to win, you are at peace and confident going forward. A story will help demonstrate my point.

When the wind blows

Years ago, a farmer who owned land along the Atlantic Ocean seacoast constantly advertised for hired hands. Most people were reluctant to work on farms along the Atlantic seacoast because of the awful storms that raged across the Atlantic, wreaking havoc on the buildings and crops. As the farmer interviewed applicants for the job, he received a steady stream of refusals. Finally a short thin man, well past middle age, approached the farmer.

"Are you a good farmhand?" the farmer asked him.

"Well, I can sleep when the wind blows," answered the old thin man.

Although puzzled by the answer, the desperate farmer hired the man. The little man worked well around the farm, busy from dawn to dusk, and the farmer was well satisfied with the man's work.

Then one night, the wind howled loudly, coming in from offshore. Jumping out of bed, the farmer grabbed a lantern and rush next door to the hired hand's sleeping quarters. He shook the little man and yelled, "Get up, a storm is on its way! Tie things down before they blow away."

The little man rolled over in bed and said firmly, "No, sir, I told you that I can sleep when the wind blows."

Enraged by the man's response, the farmer was tempted to fire him on the spot. Instead, he hurried outside to prepare for the storm. To his amazement, he discovered that all the haystacks had been covered with tarpaulins. The cows were in the barn, the chickens were in their coops, the doors were barred, the shutters were secured tightly, everything was tied down firmly and efficiently. Nothing could blow away!

The farmer then understood what his hired hand meant, so he returned to his bed to also "sleep when the wind blows!"

The obvious moral to this story is: when you are prepared, spiritually, mentally, and physically, you have nothing to fear. Can you sleep when the wind blows? Are you prepared?

In the gospel of Matthew 11:28–29, our Lord reminds us, "Come to me all you who labor and are heavy laden, and I will give you rest. Take my yoke upon you and learn from Me, for I am gentle and lowly in heart, and you will find rest for your souls."

As a coach, one has to prepare not only his players but his coaching staff as well. You cannot do it alone; you must have competent people that are on the same page as you are. We always began to meet as a staff in the winter months before summer workouts began. That way, by the time summer practices began, we were all working together with the same techniques and schemes. Great programs create an environment where competition is present at practice to make all involved more fervent and passionate about the outcome. The more perspicacious those involved are, the keener the team is at executing the game plan.

THE COAT OF MANY COLORS

Joseph had a coat of many colors, and he wore it with pride. His brothers saw him in it and were offended by his insensitivity toward them, and they were jealous of their father's affection for Joseph. Joseph would strut around in his coat, and their anger would burn. "Let us slay him and cast him into some pit, we will say to our father some beast has devoured him, then we shall see what becomes of his dreams."

"Behold here comes, the dreamer." They nicknamed him Dreamer, and little did they know, at the time, that the title would be accurate in their future and Joseph's to save their family and the nation of Israel during a severe famine. It was not meant as a positive statement but a put-down, but what man intended for bad, God meant for good.

Many teams in football have nicknames for their teammates as well; they are often referred to by qualities or characteristics that are unique to them: size, speed, looks, abilities, and other distinct characteristics. The only nicknames I don't care for are the negative ones that are meant to hurt or demean. Joseph's brothers were planning on killing him and telling their father a made-up story about "the dreamer." The world always has a negative twist to spin on the nickname, but God will use that name to accomplish his purposes, not the world's. As they said in Genesis 37:20, "We shall see what will become of his dreams." The older brother Reuben said, "Let's not kill him…but cast him into a pit in the wilderness, and lay no hand upon him." Reuben had the idea of going back to rescue Joseph later, though he did not have the courage to say what he really wanted to do. So they cast Joseph into the pit, and there was no water or food there. What do you suppose was going on in Joseph's mind at that time? His dream were shattered, and he was now isolated from all. There was nothing he could do but *pray to God!*

Joseph now had to take responsibility for his own actions and stop blaming everyone else—brothers, parents, society—for his situation.

God was with him, and God would provide the comfort, if he sought the comforter. His brothers were sitting down to eat when their conscience began to speak to them, "Come let us sell him the Ishmaelites, and let us not put our hand upon him, for he is our brother and our flesh, and they were content." Imagine that; they were able to be at peace, and they had just sold their brother into slavery? Mankind can be so selfish and cruel to one another.

The "Banquet Table" story is an example of man's hardness of heart versus self-sacrifice.

Many years ago, an old man died and went to visit hell. His guide walked with him into a room with a giant banquet table covered with sumptuous food and delicacies of many varieties. Roasted beef, chicken, pork, fish, and other wonderful prepared dishes, also desserts and sweets that surpassed one's imagination. The air was filled with the best-smelling food that ever graced a table. Surprised by what he saw, there were seated around the banquet table many inhabitants with long faces, malnourished, wane, and emaciated faces. They were angry because try as they might, they could not get the food into their mouths. Their hands were extremely long spoons that extended across the table toward their fellow banqueters. The food remained uneaten, and the guests were livid with anger, and starvation was an unending consequence. Hell was filled with the hungry, tortured by the fact that as close to the most amazing food imaginable, they would never eat it!

The guide then took the man to visit heaven and found the same scenario of setting with a spectacular banquet table and sumptuous food.

The guests here also had extremely long spoons for hands, and they, too, extended across there table where they sat. However, there was profound difference. The souls in heaven sat across from each other, not trying to feed themselves but rather trying to feed the person sitting across from them. Their faces were bright, happy, and nourished by the food. They were healthy, strong, and joyful because they were content with helping one another, not just themselves. What a beautiful vision the old man thought, as he viewed the scene. What a place to spend eternity. You see, the real difference between heaven and hell is that the inhabitants of hell are only concerned about themselves, where in heaven, people spend their time serving each other. We, too, can make a difference here on earth by making our lives an extension of heaven or a reflection of hell. Do you concern yourself with the needs of others, or are you only concerned about yourself and your wants?

Joseph was in a situation where he had to pray for God's protection and mercy. Despite his brothers' cruelty and intentions, God's hand was watching over him each day, and God had a plan much larger than Joseph could imagine. A plan that included Joseph helping his brothers, his family, and the entire people of Israel. The brothers lifted Joseph out of the pit and sold him to the Ishmaelites. They brought him into Egypt where a new life awaited Joseph. Joseph would always remember how he was lifted out of the pit; he knew God was with him. He had seen God act, and he would never forget that. He did not get a chance to say goodbye to his father; he could only say it in his heart.

Suddenly Joseph was in a strange new country. The Ishmaelites sold him to a high-ranking officer in the Egyptian Army, a man named Potiphar. Now Joseph had gone through a lot but still had a lot to deal with in the future. God knows what we can handle and allowed Joseph to experience a positive relationship with Potiphar. He needed to learn the graces and manners of a new culture, and his mentor would be Potiphar. Potiphar was a man of class, wealth, and prestige. Joseph watched and learned from Potiphar the nuances of Egyptian culture; he used him as a role model. Joseph was allowed to live in his master's home, not in the slave quarters nearby. Even though Joseph started at the bottom, he knew that the Lord was with him. More importantly, Potiphar saw that the Lord was with Joseph, and he must have been told by Joseph about Yahweh, his God, because Potiphar was an unbeliever. Joseph must have shared his relationship with God to Potiphar. Potiphar recognized something different about Joseph, and he liked it, but he also would observe Joseph to see what this God was like.

Joseph was unattached to Egypt, which allowed him to be at peace despite the unfamiliar surroundings. Joseph's main ambition was to be vindicated in his brothers' eyes, something that was currently an unattainable goal. God would work out his plan, in his timing, and for his purposes. Potiphar was experiencing wealth and good fortune especially, because of Joseph's presence. Joseph had been faithful in Potiphar's house. One day Potiphar's wife cast her eyes on Joseph who was well built and handsome. She made a move toward him, for which he was not prepared. Here is the young Joseph, in charge of the entire household of Potiphar, being the target of sexual overtones. Potiphar's wife said one day, "I've got to have Joseph." Potiphar trusted Joseph, because he knew how much Joseph loved his God.

Joseph responded to her by saying, "How can I do this wickedness and sin against God?" He could not sin against God, and God would remember that and be with him through all his trials. Potiphar was enraged at the accusation his wife made, and there was nothing Joseph could do to defend himself. He had to keep his mouth shut because no one would believe him anyway.

This is another great example of Joseph for us, not being in control of a situation. If we try to defend ourselves, we will often be in a bigger mess than when we started; we will look foolish. However, God says if we trust in him and be quiet, He will be moved and will act on our behalf. He will be our vindicator. I am going to step in and take care of you. I know from the incident in 2012, at Huron, that I cannot act on my own behalf, but God has. People I barely know have said words of encouragement to me regarding the entire event; it is amazing at times. Joseph did four things when tempted by Potiphar's wife:

1. "My master does not concern himself with anything in his house; everything he has entrusted to my care." He valued Potiphar's trust and feelings.
2. "There is none greater in this house of Potiphar's than me. He has kept nothing back from me." He had self-respect.
3. He respected Potiphar's wife by saying, "You are his wife.". He showed unselfish love and respect for her and himself. He did not give in to lust.
4. "How can I do this wickedness and sin against God?" "You shall not commit adultery" came years later, but Joseph acted it out in the present.

He also repeatedly said no to her advances, not just once or twice but every day. Strength is not just resisting temptation; true strength is refusing to go where temptation will be. The most difficult test that a person might have to face if he or she is to be used by God is to be punished for doing right and then be patient and let God step in and defend us in his own timing, not ours. Jesus was not defended during his passion and death, despite the fact that he asked the Father, "Take this cup from Me, not My will but Thy will be done." He may have lost the battle, but he definitely won the war. Jesus could have come down from the cross and destroyed all his enemies, struck them dead, while the mobs shouted, "If you are the Son of God, come down from the cross." He would have won the battle and lost the war. Now Joseph was in a similar situation in that God was preparing him for something much greater—the saving of his people during a famine. Joseph had already experienced God's protection with Potiphar's favor and benevolence in his house. He was now going to see it again with the keeper of the prison, who was impressed with what he saw in Joseph. Joseph was prospering again by being put in charge of all the prisoners, not a goal he had in life, but he was about to win the war if he remained patient. God gave favor to Joseph despite his circumstances, despite his predicaments and false accusations.

We, too, will experience his presence as we wait patiently for him to manifest our victory over sin and death.

I have prayed for God to vindicate me as a result of the incident, but what is more important is his objective being made apparent rather than my concerns. Those directly involved know all the facts, and some have lied or kept quiet despite knowing the truth. I know in the final analysis, God will act in his time for his purposes. I have taken responsibility for my actions and know that never was there an intention to cause embarrassment of the opposition. We simply played with intensity and pride, seeking to improve weekly. If you don't play football with that intent, then you may as well not play at all. We lost many starters that season with injuries and still managed to win the league championship of the SEC.

When you lose a QB, it is difficult to excel when each week, there was a different starting secondary unit to prepare and when all the members of the coaching staff had not bought into the program and the kids' best interests; winning is extremely challenging. Yet we still played in the district championship and won decisively the first round of the playoffs against a good Monroe team, 31–0, while allowing only 7.2 points per game in League play. I am very grateful to the student athletes on the 2012 Pioneer squad for their compassion that they demonstrated in the final game of the regular season against Livonia Franklin and the first-round playoff game against Monroe. Many kids taped my name to their helmets in a show of respect, and all of them played with intensity throughout both games. Unfortunately when I did return in the district final, I was too lethargic in our preparation and got outcoached by our opponent. I was just happy to be back and lost my focus and intensity. We also lost one of our starting RBs due to some personal issues he was facing that I should have handled better, but the stress from the previous three weeks took a toll, and I did not keep my priorities in line. The RB we lost was the only player to score a TD in our first meeting against Saline in week 4, a game we won despite five to six turnovers. Attention to detail is so important in football, the ultimate team game. As Bo said, "The team, the team, the team!"

After Joseph was in prison for some time, he interpreted the dreams of the Pharaoh's butler and his baker, in prison. The butler was restored to his position after three days, and the baker was hanged, just as Joseph had predicted. God was in control, but as Joseph was speaking to the butler and the baker, he added to his interpretation, "But think of me when it is well with you, and show kindness to me I pray." Joseph thought it wise to call attention to himself, but God taught Joseph a deeper lesson, that he could do what he predicted without Joseph's help. Although God could have freed Joseph immediately, he chose to allow him to be incarcerated another two years to get him to the place God wanted him to be at.

We often say, "I cannot take any more," but God will never put us through more than we can handle. He knows us better than we know ourselves. He works all things together for good to those whom he loves and are called according to his purpose. Joseph wanted to be restored, but the butler forgot that Joseph had interpreted his dream and brought him back to the Pharaoh's presence in the palace. So the butler forgot about Joseph, and Joseph was waiting for a knock on the prison door that did not come. God wanted to do it his way.

Humble yourself before the mighty hand of God, that He may exalt you in due time.

God says, "I want to do it, I want to get involved with you and show you my love and compassion." At the end of two years, the Pharaoh had a dream, and who would have considered that the ruler of Egypt would have a dream about a Hebrew prisoner? Actually the Pharaoh had two dreams; he was very upset by the dreams, so he called in his wise men, or astrologers, to interpret the dreams for him. One after another, they said they did not have a clue what the dreams meant. When the common explanation fails, then it is time for God to act, and act he did.

Most of us take vindication into our own hands, and sometimes we succeed, but it is actually a compliment God pays you when you try and fail to vindicate yourself. God is saying, "I am going to take care of you and this situation." There is another indication that God's time has come, and that is when someone else pleads your case without you even opening your mouth—silenzio/silence. I hope and pray that God will vindicate those who are seeking the truth.

> Pharaoh sent for Joseph and they brought him hastily out
> of the dungeon.

The Gospel tells us that we can be saved when we come to the end of our own strength and allow God to be God, our Savior!

Joseph had been in anything but a salubrious environment: a pit, a slave caravan, a sexual accusation, and a dungeon. Now the leader of one of the most powerful countries on earth at the time was inviting him into the palace for dream interpretation. The Pharaoh said to Joseph, "I have dreamed a dream and nobody can help me, all else has failed but I am told that you can help."

Joseph answered, "It is not me, my God shall give you an answer of peace."

The Pharaoh believed his butler, and now he also believed Joseph. The king related his dream, Joseph listened, then gave the king explicit advice. The end result was the Pharaoh said, "Can we find a man such as this man, a man in whom the Spirit of God dwells?" Pharaoh believed Joseph's interpretation for one reason—Joseph had the Spirit of God in him. There was no way that the Pharaoh could immediately prove whether he had made the right decision in trusting Joseph's interpretation. It took fourteen years to prove that Joseph was right.

Yet somehow, the Pharaoh knew that he had made the right choice; the Spirit of God was at work in him, and it gave him peace, the peace that Joseph had promised God would provide. We, too, experience peace when we don't just look for answers in the physical realm, sight, touch, smell, taste, and sounds. We all have tried to make our sensual experiences the foremost important reality in our lives, but it is fleeting and temporary at best. Music we listened to growing up, we thought was inspired, but often who was it inspired by? Tactile stimulation was exciting, but it was momentary and transient. Visual beauty is exhilarating but ephemeral and often leads to lust. The scent of a field of lavender is an aromatic bouquet for a time. A sumptuous meal can stimulate our savory taste buds, but we can also pig out and be miserable. Only the spiritual realm gives lasting satisfaction, peace, a sense of calmness, an assurance of being in God's presence, of choosing right over wrong, of choosing where we hope to spend eternity. Sexual dynamics are exciting to most of us, and God intended it to be so, but he intended sex for the marriage union, not anywhere at any time, with any one or more of either sexes. He allows us to choose; claiming an abused phrase, he made us pro-choice. He gave us freedom from the beginning. We are free, in a sense, to do whatever we want with our bodies; however, we are not free to determine whether what we do with our bodies is good or evil. Therefore, human freedom, "choice," is fully realized not by inventing good and evil but by choosing properly between them.

Certainly forced love is not love at all; that is why we have the freedom to choose to love God or not. Even Lucifer had the freedom to choose whether to worship God or not, and he chose to place himself above God in his own mind, just as many of us do. "I will rise above the throne of the most high God," this is what Lucifer said, the most beautiful angel God created. Now the devil tries to entice us to put ourselves first, too, to have boastful pride and indulge our every sense. There is a difference between love and lust.

God created us male and female from the beginning. He saw that it was not good for man to be alone (although man had solitude with God) and created woman as his mate or partner. It is a spiritual union as well, not just a physical union. Communion of man and woman and the procreation of a child is a good example of the spiritual unity of God, the Father, the Son, and the Holy Spirit. God created us male and female, and they were naked before sin entered our existence. They felt no shame or lust because they were fully committed and totally given to each other. Pope John Paul II says that this love between Adam and Eve was like a fully inflated tire. It allowed them to love unconditionally, to ride smoothly through life. With the onset of sin, original sin, their tires began to lose air rapidly, and they were riding on the rims most of the time.

Sin caused them to feel shame in their nakedness. God intended for man and woman to be a gift to one another, freely given, and to be fruitful and multiply. Sin brought a selfish element to their sexual intimacy; their tires needed to be inflated, not deflated. Only in heaven will they be fully inflated, but we can experience a smoother ride as we give ourselves to one another completely and draw closer to Jesus Christ in this world.

Despite sin, Jesus came to restore mankind to their original holiness. We cannot return to that state of innocence, but we can progress on the journey, keeping our tires as full as possible along the way.

Pharaoh affirmed Joseph right away when Joseph interpreted his dreams. He said, "It is good in the eyes of the Pharaoh and in the eyes of all his servants." Joseph put himself on the spot with his advice and the specificity of his interpretation. They would all know within a year or so whether he was correct or not. If there was not an abundance of rain, sun, and vegetation with good soil, he would prove the fool. He would be living in disgrace the rest of his life. However, Pharaoh was the one who risked even more by listening and trusting a foreigner, a slave, while he ruled the most powerful nation on earth. Joseph then added advice that the Pharaoh should prepare for the years of famine by appointing a wise discerning man over the land of Egypt. As it turned out, Joseph's predictions were true, and God showed that he was truly in control of all that was going on, including Joseph's life. Pharaoh put his ring on Joseph's hand, arrayed him in fine linen, put a gold chain around his neck, and made him to sit in the second chariot while all of Egypt paid him homage. Joseph had finally come home, and home was not where he was but when he was destined for glory. God used all the circumstances that preceded his being made governor of Egypt to put him in this position. God does move in mysterious ways. God also provided a wife for Joseph in Egypt, something he had not anticipated at all. Egypt was so blessed the first seven years that they stopped keeping record of all their harvest; it was so plentiful. They stored the food for future years as Joseph had recommended.

Joseph's brothers were sent to Egypt to inquire about food during the famine in Israel. Joseph would be tested to see how he would react to his brothers.

This past weekend, I attended the forty-year reunion of the 1976 National Football Champions, the University of Pittsburgh. I drove down with the father of a current player at Pitt, Nate Bossary, with his father, Mike. It was super seeing teammates from forty years ago, having dinner, talking, telling old war stories, and watching Pitt defeat Penn State University at Heinz Field in Pittsburgh. *How my brothers would receive me?* was on my mind when we drove down. Memories of past wrongs, hurts, deeds of kindness, and sweating through workouts, as well as hits and plays on and off the field. I soon found a warm reception from my teammates, a common recognition from them of my former years and previous interactions, as well as recognition of my present status. There were no sour attitudes exhibited from past wrongs, just love and respect.

I am sure Joseph, in Genesis, felt the same when he encountered his brothers that had sold him into slavery years ago and sought to kill him at one point. My brother in the Lord and great friend Ron Medley was there, and we have always had each other's back, literally and figuratively. We roomed together and talked until 3:00 a.m., of the present and the past. I believe Joseph only wanted to embrace his brothers and demonstrate forgiveness toward them, despite what they had done to him. He saved them and the nation of Israel from famine and restored them and his father in his presence.

Tony Dorsett was the star of our team, the Heisman winner of 1976 and eventual NFL Hall of Fame running back. It was he that the media sought to interview and focus their cameras on, and who could blame them, he was "the man" at Pitt. They named a street after him near the stadium. The years that have gone by moved almost as fast as he ran on the field. Speed and great vision were his MO. He is the ninth leading rusher of all time in the NFL.

This following weekend, I had the pleasure of attending a reunion at School Tech in Ann Arbor, owned by the Canham family for years. Don Eaton and his family were our hosts. Bob Stites, the president of the M Club, was there to greet many of his former teammates at U of M.

The evening focused around celebrating Coach Bill McCartney's time at U of M as Bo Schembechler's defensive coordinator in the '70s and early '80s. He then became the head coach at the University of Colorado in 1981. There, he had incredible success defeating the great Oklahoma and Nebraska teams of that era. CU was the opponent for Michigan that Saturday at the Big House. I saw many former athletes that I had met over the years, including Stanley Edwards, Mike Hardin, and Fred Brockington. Stan, Mike, and I worked at Sandy Sanders football camp together in the early '80s. The current assistant director of the MHSAA, Nate Hampton, also worked this camp, and we were roommates. I was playing a cassette tape of the Stylistics, very low to keep from waking Nate up. He said, "Hey, can you turn that up some?"

I said sure and enjoyed the amazing voices of Russell Tompkins Jr. and company. Coach Mac was greeted by everyone there, as players and their families waited to hug and encourage Coach Mac. He greeted me warmly and said, "Tall Paul, you haven't changed a bit, I love you."

"I love you, too, Coach, you have been a father to me, thanks." I told him about my trip to Pittsburgh the previous week, and he smiled his approval.

His son Mike and his family were there as well, and I enjoyed seeing Mike for the first time in over thirty-five years. He is an agent for professional athletes in the Chicago area. His younger brother, Tom, is a teacher and coach in the Boulder, Colorado community. Mac lost his wife, Lyndi, a few years ago, and I know he misses her greatly. I had a wonderful time at the reunion of U of M athletes. My good friend and fellow church member at Saint Andrew's of Saline, Marty Bodnar, and his twin brother, Mark, were there. I had the pleasure of meeting Mark for the first time.

Marty was an academic All-American basketball player at U of M in the 1979–1981 seasons. Former teacher and coach Dave McCarney from Ann Arbor Saint Francis, Saint Thomas was there, as was Coach Mike Coletta from Belleville. Coach Tirrel Burton and his wife were there; he truly was a gentleman and a great coach at his time at Michigan, as the running backs' coach. Coach Gary Barnett, former head coach at Northwestern and McCartney's offensive coordinator at Colorado, was there. I had the good fortune to meet him at Northwestern when I visited friend Ron Vanderlinden, his defensive coordinator at NU. Vandy and I were roommates, along with Jerry Meter, on Seventh Avenue back in the early '80s. They were both grad assistants for Bo. Meter was an outside linebacker for U of M in the late '70s and cocaptain of the team, and all Big 10. Time goes by quickly; especially as we get older, we realize how special the time that we have here is. There is a season for everything and a time for every season under heaven.

Here we are in the winter of 2018, January, and I am going back to work at M Den and coaching once again at Saline High School. Last season, I worked with the DBs at Saline, along with Coach Dunny and Coach Brown. Our defensive coordinator was Duane Wilson, and the head coach was Joe Palka.

We had eighteen coaches on the varsity, and the kids were hardworking and focused. We were SEC champs but lost in the first round of the playoffs. We lost four starters to ACL knee tears and still managed a successful season. I enjoyed getting back on the field. I also helped Coach Gene Gennoe at Monroe Jefferson High School, meeting with him and his staff. I spent quite a few hours on the phone and HUDL with Coach Ben Kohlstadt at Sanderson High School in Raleigh, North Carolina. They made it to round 3 in the playoffs, losing to the eventual 4A state champs Wake Forest High School. I really did more game planning with Sanderson than I did at Saline, where I was an assistant.

Mark Langkos ran an FCA group (Fellowship of Christian Athletes) on Tuesday mornings, and many young boys and girls benefited from his leadership.

I would like to conclude with my interaction with Coach Ben Kohlstadt in Raleigh, North Carolina. Our daughter, Andrea, and her family live in Clayton, North Carolina. We have been traveling yearly to spend time with her and the grandchildren. I met with Coach Kohlstadt in 2013 when a former Ann Arbor Pioneer, Steve Powers, was his defensive coordinator.

Steve played for us in 1985–1986. He has been in Houston, Texas, most of his career as a coach. Steve's family moved to Raleigh, North Carolina, for one year, and Steve coached with Ben at Sanderson High School. Coach Kohlstadt was hired at Leesville Road High School in 2019. They have been very competitive. I enjoy working over the phone and on HUDL in helping Ben with his defensive game plans. They were state runners-up in Division 4AA in 2019, losing to Chambers High School (formerly Zebulon Vance). Julius Chambers was a long-term civil rights attorney. Vance was a Confederate military officer during the Civil War and a slave owner.

A message is sent to the history of North Carolina. Again, we are speaking to the issue of "all men are created equal in the sight of God."

The *Ann Arbor News* did an article in 2001 called "Coaches Color Blind." Chuck Lorri, Chris Westfall, Andy Turner, Rob Eanes, Jim Dick, and I were pictured coaching together. All had coached at both Pioneer and Huron. Purple, green, and gold—they were Ann Arbor kids, regardless of color. Huron led the area on offense and defense, number 1 in both.

May we strive for M. L. K.'s quest to be judged by our "character," not our color! All equal in God's eyes!

www.ingramcontent.com/pod-product-compliance
Lightning Source LLC
Chambersburg PA
CBHW051202120626
46547CB00012B/1175